DON'T SAVE FOR RETIREMENT

A Millennial's
Guide to
Financial Freedom

DON'T SAVE

FOR

RETIREMENT

DANIEL AMEDURI

LIONCREST
PUBLISHING

DON'T SAVE FOR RETIREMENT

A Millennial's Guide to Financial Freedom

ISBN   978-1-5445-1376-8 *Paperback*
       978-1-5445-1375-1 *Ebook*

This book is dedicated to those who seek freedom. Break the chains, own your time, live your passion, and never accept another's perception of life as your reality.

All proceeds from this book will be donated to The Whale Sanctuary Project. For more information about this organization dedicated to creating seaside sanctuaries for orcas and beluga whales, visit whalesanctuaryproject.org.

CONTENTS

DISCLAIMER

The author has made every effort to ensure that the information in this book is correct at press time. The author does not assume and hereby disclaims any liability to any party for any loss, damage, or disruption caused by errors or omissions, whether such errors or omissions result from negligence, accident, or any other cause. This book is not intended to provide specific financial or legal advice. The author and *Future Money Trends* do not assume and hereby disclaim any liability to any party for any loss, damage, or disruption caused by the information in this book. For advice on your specific financial situation, please contact a qualified expert.

INTRODUCTION

I was twenty-seven when my wife, Jewel, and I sat in a lawyer's office to discuss our bankruptcy options. By that point, I had amassed a small fortune working in the Southern California real estate market since I was eighteen. Our high-end Newport Beach property had recently been featured on *Flip That House*. This property was our biggest investment to date. It was also the investment that was now tanking us.

My wife cried as the lawyer spoke. His mouth was moving, but all I could hear echoing in my ears were her protests from only an hour earlier in the car. She didn't want to file bankruptcy. Our Tennessee duplex, nice and neat and paid off, would be gone if we filed. The duplex was her last hope, and so it was mine, too.

We didn't file for bankruptcy that day, nor did we ever

consider it again. We regrouped and looked forward, as we always do.

WHAT MILLENNIALS WERE TAUGHT

I've been interested in entrepreneurship my whole life, dating back to when I was a child. Ask my mom to tell you a story from my childhood, and she'll describe the morning she woke up to find countless cars driving slowly past our house, as the passengers checked out our family's belongings, which I had removed from the garage and neatly arranged in our driveway. I sat there with my cash box, the sole proprietor of this makeshift garage sale at seven years old.

Or maybe my mom would tell you about the time my uncle, who worked for Nabisco, gave us a bunch of cookies. I proceeded to throw them into my red Radio Flyer and hawked them door to door. In fifth grade, I out-bargained my teacher, who was selling pencils to my classmates for ten cents apiece. I asked my mom for pencils and sold them for nine cents.

I've always been fascinated with money, but I've never been materialistic. My parents couldn't afford name-brand clothes or expensive jewelry, so these things never became a priority for me. I've never cared about having the biggest house or the fanciest car. I bought a Sea-Doo when I was eighteen, and that still stands out as my biggest spending mistake. I am fortunate that I was never sidetracked by the materialistic needs that drive so many.

At thirteen, I started reading personal finance books. I came across a book by financial guru Robert T. Kiyosaki entitled *If You Want to Be Rich & Happy Don't Go to School: Ensuring Lifetime Security for Yourself and Your Children*. As a teenager sitting in the finance section of Barnes & Noble, a self-help book written by an expert telling me *not* to go to school was not only mesmerizing, it was life-changing.

When you know you want to learn how to make money at a young age, but everyone tells you that you first need things you don't have the money to get—like a college degree—the world can feel pretty overwhelming. It's like applying for your first credit card: you need good credit to get approved, but you can't establish that credit without a credit card.

Thirteen was a big year for me. I began studying martial arts at a local studio. My instructor was a wealthy man, who taught me about so much more than the ins and outs of karate. We talked about the stock market, different company trends, and the value of buying during those periods when everyone else is scared. We talked about how important it is to purchase rental properties instead of a single-family house so that you can live in one of the units and rent out the others for income. Of course, I would have to grow up, try his tactics, and make my own mistakes before I *really* learned what it took to be wealthy.

I was sixteen when I became a partial owner of the martial arts studio along with that instructor, who went on to become my mentor both in martial arts and in life. Legally, my father was the owner of my 25 percent share of the studio, but I acted as the owner and manager on a daily basis. I registered students and closed sales contracts, all while learning about business and money.

When I was working at the studio, I felt motivated and encouraged. School just didn't cut it for me. I enrolled in a home economics class, simply because I was one of only two guys among thirty students. You can't beat those odds anywhere. Despite my ulterior motives, I did manage to pay attention to a few things in that home ec class. For example, one day the teacher showed us a graph demonstrating the difference in income between a high school graduate and the average college graduate. At that time, in the mid-1990s, a high school graduate made $25,000 a year. Not too impressive, even then. But what was truly underwhelming was that college graduates made only $10,000 more. *Ten thousand*. I couldn't believe it. As the teacher proudly displayed these numbers, thinking she was showing us the importance of a college degree, I sat in my chair, staring at the screen. *Either way, I'm so screwed*, I thought. I needed a different path.

It was at this point I knew I was never going to college. The problem was that everyone in my life expected me to go—my father, my mother, my school counselors, even my future in-laws. In fact, I was the first person in my family to graduate from high school.

My parents accepted whatever path I chose, but for my future (now current) in-laws, college is as important as religion, and I didn't want to upset them. I decided to tell my in-laws that I was attending East Los Angeles College, and I kept up this charade for a year. What I was actually doing was going to Barnes & Noble, roaming up and down the business, finance, and self-help aisles, and reading about economics, investments, personal finance, and real estate. I read every one of the yellow books for dummies in finance, and every Tony Robbins book about personal development.

If you're searching for your life's purpose, go to a bookstore and notice the section where you could sit down and pull books from the shelves all day long. That's where you want to be.

It wasn't long before I tried to purchase a rental property.

This isn't an easy feat for an eighteen-year-old to pull off, but I didn't know that. I was turned down by four or five different loan officers and passed over by the same number of realtors before I met Virginia. Virginia was an eighty-year-old real estate broker who was willing to help a kid out. She was the kind of person who wanted to give everyone a shot. This applied even to people who were trying to do something unconventional and seemingly impossible. Everyone should look out for the Virginias in their life.

At eighteen, I bought my first condo and rented it to a family of four. The couple was in their forties or fifties, with two teenagers who were only three years younger than me. I was so intimidated that I told them I was the landlord's nephew. That way, I could talk about my scary uncle who liked the rent on time without feeling like I lacked authority.

I purchased a second condo six months later, in what became my first creative real estate financing deal. After proving myself to Virginia, I worked with her again, this time borrowing her commission of $10,000 up front and taking a lien on my first condo to buy the second.

I was officially up and running in the real estate market in the 2000s, cashing in on the largest bubble in US real estate history.

It was easy to confuse the luck I was experiencing with know-how. Don't get me wrong, I was doing the right thing by learning all I could and getting involved in real estate early. But when you're nineteen and making $10,000 a month in equity on real estate appreciation, it's easy to forget all the luck you've encountered. You think you're smart and that everything you touch will turn to gold. It took seven years of riding high for me to crash hard when I tried to sneak in a few more big flips and real estate purchases before the bubble burst.

THE CRASH

It was frustrating. I could see the trends happening in markets all over the country, but especially in Southern California, where Jewel and I had lived our entire lives. I even started a YouTube channel based on my market predictions, but, at the time, I thought my last big purchases would allow us to cash up for the downturn. I didn't fully understand the magnitude of the situation. Whereas we'd never used credit cards to pay for anything, we were now paying all our mortgages and investment properties' monthly expenses on credit. Once I sold, cashed out most of my early sales, then reinvested all the money back in the real estate market in 2007, almost everything fore-closed or was in a short sale. I lost almost everything I ever made. My luck ran out, and whatever destiny I once thought I had in building wealth was erased.

For the first time in my life, I wasn't investing or actively involved in any business. I wasn't even thinking about real estate. The foreclosures kept rolling in. If you've ever foreclosed on a home, you know the stress and pressure it causes. Now multiply that by eight. We were foreclosing on eight homes and defaulting on five different credit cards, all at the same time. The phone calls and visits from debt collectors were overwhelming. I gave up. But I didn't go bankrupt.

STARTING OVER

I didn't know how to make money in a down market. While Jewel went to work as a teacher during the day, I stayed home and slept. There was no way around it; I was depressed. I jumped at any opportunity to make money outside of investments, just so I could feel like I was the partner my wife deserved. I spent sixty days earning a Class A license in truck driving school, even though I'd never so much as driven a stick shift in my life. Then I started stocking shelves for twelve dollars an hour at the local grocery store at night. At least it was something.

For all the mistakes I made, I did some things right. We immediately stopped using our credit cards and implemented a cash system, dividing up our cash for the week into envelopes labeled for specific expenses, like "groceries" or "gas." We sold our house in Upland and rented a home in the desert. We raised goats and chickens in an effort to live a more sustainable lifestyle, and we even gave our special needs dogs to a warm and loving dachshund rescue. Our entire mindset had shifted. We didn't want to be rich anymore—we just didn't want to be poor.

I began to look at money and wealth differently. I was no longer focused on the paper wealth that makes you feel good for a while. Instead, I began to value the type of wealth that comes from having peace of mind.

When our son was born in 2009, Jewel wanted to stay home with him. She wanted to have the time to raise him and enjoy his childhood instead of giving all her attention to other people's kids in the classroom. I wanted to be the kind of dad who didn't have to sacrifice sleep just to spend a little time with my son. I also didn't want to pay a sitter so I could get some sleep during the hours while my wife worked.

A MODEL FOR THRIVING IN THE NEW ECONOMY

Jewel and I used to enjoy dinners out with a nice bottle of wine, but that didn't matter anymore. We became even more aggressive about cutting our expenses, and set our sights on achieving a level of financial independence that would allow my wife to stay home. This meant facing my fears and diving back into the financial world. At Jewel's urging, I started Vision Victory, my first YouTube channel focused on financial trends. I had only a twenty-dollar Logitech webcam at my disposal, but it did the job. Within six months, Google took over YouTube and I was making money. My hobby had become my profession.

I found my way out of dire financial straits thanks to a mindset shift about two things: wealth and reprioritizing those things that were most important in my life. I noticed that principles that always interested me—like entrepreneurship and making my own way—were gaining traction in the world, especially among millennials. I loved the idea of being a freelancer rather than an employee. I also loved the notion that financial independence can be achieved younger than ever before through basic lifestyle changes and adjusting antiquated notions of wealth. All this became the foundation of my eventual newsletter, *Future Money Trends*, and the inspiration for this book. This is now my multi-million-dollar business.

I wanted the newsletter (and, later, my business) to focus on the new economy. It was clear to me that the portfolio and personal finance model was broken, even for baby boomers. I wanted to show people in my generation how to navigate the new economic environment. The 2008 crisis was hard on a lot of people, including me. I found a way out, and a way to rebuild, and I had to share it. This book is yet another step in sharing this information. Information that can change how you look at work, money, and life.

This isn't a get-rich-quick book. I've read enough of those in my lifetime to know that I have no interest in showing you how to afford a private jet or live a yacht-vacation lifestyle. Penny stocks aren't my thing, and I'm no expert in starting a business. I do know that our economy has changed and will change again. Our problem is that we fail at adjusting our lifestyles and expectations to these changes.

Whether you make $35,000 or $100,000, the time is right to start working toward financial freedom. This means a life in which you call the shots, no matter what. Maybe you'll use this knowledge to become a millionaire in five to ten years. Or maybe you'll embrace a new lifestyle so *you* are in charge of your future, your security, and your happiness. Either way, by applying the strategies in this book, you'll understand what wealth means to you.

Throughout this book, you'll discover spending pitfalls, why retirement is an outdated experiment that ultimately failed, and how multiple streams of revenue create passive income and a sustainable life. We will discuss the freelance economy, risk assessment, and cryptocurrency investment. I've tested every suggestion and recommendation I will make to you. You can rest assured that I've made every single mistake I will point out to you and grappled with and overcome every fear you might be facing.

The discoveries I've made have transformed my life. I'm confident that they will do the same for you.

CHAPTER ONE

THE CONCEPT OF WEALTH

In the end, money should serve something greater than just money. It should serve you, your family, the people you want to touch.

—TONY ROBBINS

From the moment we have even a small understanding of money, most of us believe that being wealthy means being financially successful. In practice, wealth means something different to each of us, and we each must undergo a personal journey to reach that understanding. I'm not someone who believes that wealth has nothing to do with money or that money cannot make us happy. Money can buy peace of mind when we eliminate debt from our lives, and that inner peace makes us healthier and happier. Someone with no debt can wake up happy in a mobile home; likewise, someone with a six-figure salary, hefty mortgage, and countless car payments can find themselves tossing and turning at night, living in fear of the future.

WHAT IS REAL WEALTH?

In my early twenties, I figured I would be wealthy when I made all the money I wanted. My thoughts were focused on finance and real estate. Between time spent with my real estate business and teaching at the martial arts studio, I worked roughly sixteen hours every day. I sold my waking hours for money, subscribing to the illusion that the money I made would lead to "wealth." What I did not realize, however, is that I would eventually lose all the money that once made me a millionaire. I would lose it all, only to get it back again. That's how money works. But that's not how time works, unfortunately. I was not able to gain back my time—time with my wife, time with my parents, even time with friends.

Now, I'm constantly reflecting and recentering. Our lives are filled with distractions, from deadlines and doctor's appointments, to bills and meetings. It's easy to lose focus on the good stuff—the important stuff. Just as we refresh and update our technology, we have to do the same for ourselves and our mindsets. How are we using our time? Are we happy?

I learned what wealth means to me when I realized that I felt complete disdain for every second I spent stocking shelves at the grocery store. I was in a dead-end job, trying to make the most of the situation but feeling like I was falling short every day. I hated that I had to work at night and that someone else was in control of my time. I hated that I had to travel around to different grocery stores for every shift and I was told where to go and when to be there. I had no control of my destiny, and I was miserable.

One of the happiest days of my life was the day when I made enough money with my YouTube channel, doing what I loved, to finally quit my job at the grocery store. I realized what it meant to be poor, and that it was not just about money. Sure, my wife and I did not have a lot of it because we were rebuilding, but that wasn't what bothered me. What bothered me was that I was giving someone else complete control of my happiness every day. The majority of my time was not mine, all for a price slightly above minimum wage. This is why Jewel and I never set our sights on having the biggest house on the water, or the fanciest car in the lot. Our ultimate goal was to be free and in control of our own lives.

A FINANCIAL TOOL AND ICON

Whether you are rich or poor, when you hit a point in life where financial wealth becomes important, it is imperative to acknowledge—and accept—what money is. Money is a financial tool that we have created as a culture. We can hold it in our hand and the government tells us we can make it and spend it as a medium of exchange, but in reality, money is significant because of the value we assign to it in our minds. Just like we all stop at a red light, we all value that piece of paper that signifies a dollar bill, or the digital values that represent our bank account.

Don't get me wrong—money is an important tool. In fact, it is probably the most important tool we can learn to leverage and strive to master in our lives. Accepting the importance and value of money as a tool means realizing that we do not need twenty different screwdrivers in our garage. Likewise, we do not need millions of dollars. What we do need, however, is the freedom to live the life we want. Money helps in the pursuit of that goal—but it is not the end goal.

KEEPING UP WITH THE JONESES

Who leads a wealthier life? A fisherman or an attorney? The fisherman goes out early in the morning and finishes his workday around lunchtime, at which point he can return home to spend the remainder of the day with his family. The attorney wakes up at six o'clock in the morning and spends all day at his office or at the courthouse. He comes home at seven o'clock and fits in a quick dinner before he begins reviewing documents for court the following day. This high-powered attorney may bring in $2 million annually while the fisherman makes $50,000, but who is ultimately wealthier? I think the fisherman lives a wealthier life—a life in which he has time with his loved ones.

There is a caveat to this, however. While our time on Earth is finite and we have to prioritize, some people gain great satisfaction from their work, and enjoy working long hours. If that is where their passion lies, they should follow it. Maybe our attorney is a prosecutor who focuses on pedophiles, and he is fulfilled by fighting for the safety and welfare of children twelve hours a day. For most of us, though, it's easy to get caught up in the vicious cycle of wanting more, and thinking we *need* more, when the answer to happiness is not the acquisition of things, but of time.

If you are in a higher income bracket, this realization can be more difficult to come to. I see it all the time at FutureMoneyTrends.com; people email me about their financial troubles when they make $200,000 a year. It's difficult to imagine that anyone who brings in that kind of money struggles financially, but when their debt is double their annual income (as it often is), life can start to feel like a burden. Doctors, lawyers, and anyone else with a high-profile career are expected to live the lifestyle of a high-profile person. Society thinks they should drive fancy cars and live in expensive houses. Before long, the higher-income earners start to agree, despite what their own common sense tells them. This is why higher-income earners typically have a more difficult time gaining financial independence than those who make $50,000 a year.

We are a culture of overspenders, no matter our income bracket. Everyone must overcome society's expectations, and everyone faces peer pressure. When I achieved millionaire status in 2013, I was driving a 2003 Nissan Altima with a few hundred thousand miles on it. I had to swallow my pride, but I loved that car and I was proud of it. It was a symbol of good decision-making and of fighting the good fight to get my life in order.

We are in a tough situation as a society. As the economy inflated, our expectations inflated, as well. The fact that we make an annual salary of $50,000 does not mean we should drive a car of that value. In reality, if we make $50,000 a year, we *should* drive a vehicle that costs no more than $5,000. I've always found it funny that we congratulate people when they buy a new car. Why do we celebrate debt? I feel that condolences are more in order—condolences for the years they lost working to pay for that car, and for the time they will never get back.

When Jewel and I moved to the desert, most people thought we had gone off the deep end. Our family and friends assumed we had either lost everything financially—which was true—or that we were taking the self-sustainable lifestyle too far—which was also true. The most important reason we moved to the desert, however, was because our mindset had changed. We were done with the peer pressure we felt to spend beyond our actual means, and we wanted something more from life than the never-ending bills and overfinanced mortgages of our friends. Most of all, we wanted to reclaim our lives and our time. While our friends moved into homes with $600,000 mortgages, we moved into a house that cost us $95,000. Sure, their homes were beautiful and their cars were luxurious; but I can't remember the last time I thought about someone's fancy new car after the first time they showed it to me. When it comes down to it, no one *really* cares about the cars that we drive or the clothes that we wear.

It's difficult to overcome peer pressure when we are young, and it is just as hard when we are older. We never learned how to manage our money in school, and we were conditioned into a certain lifestyle by our parents, based on how they were raised. When we look and act poor but we're not, we have to be confident—confident that the road less traveled truly is the most fruitful road in the end. We may look like a failure, but we know real wealth is within our reach when we change our mindset.

WHAT MAKES YOU HAPPY?

Some of the most successful entrepreneurs of all time—people like Steve Jobs and Walt Disney—did not care about making a dime. They cared about building a dream. Dreams don't have to be business empires, either. To me, dreams are about whatever makes us feel happy and fulfilled. I want to be home with my three kids and be able to travel with them when we want. It's simple, but that's what makes me happy.

From time to time, my son asks me if I want to become a billionaire. When you are a family who is transparent about finances, it's easy for young minds to focus on riches. My goal has never been to become a billionaire, but I'm not against it—I don't think anybody is. Most billionaires, however, get there by accident. Jeff Bezos, Amazon's founder and CEO, did not start Amazon with the idea that it would make him rich. Instead, he wanted to create an online bookstore that sold books at discounted prices, and the money followed. Most millionaires and billionaires do not sit around counting their stacks of money. They follow their dreams and use the resultant money as a financial tool to achieve their lifestyle. When we discuss personal finance at Future-MoneyTrends.com, we focus on how we can keep the same career—if that's what makes us happy—but live the life we want to live.

My wife and I have traveled side-by-side in this journey of amassing great fortune, losing everything, and finding ourselves—and our priorities—again. You'll get the chance to hear her side of the story throughout the book in Jewel's Corner.

JEWEL'S CORNER: REAL WEALTH

Real wealth is being financially independent and happy. Some people have a lot of money but suffer in their relationships with their spouse and children. I think your immediate family and your relationships are the most precious things you can have. Don't neglect your spouse or kids—they are the biggest blessings. Money comes and goes, but the investment you make into your relationships will become your cornerstone.

We should constantly reflect on our lives and figure out what makes us happy. What do we want to achieve? All the money in the world will not buy happiness, so we must work on adjusting our mindset for the day when we do have money; that way, we can use it as the tool it is meant to be.

Goal-setting should never include reaching a certain dollar amount. A goal of $50,000 quickly turns into $100,000, then $500,000 and $1 million. One of the biggest problems with making money is that once we have it, we want more. Life becomes a never-ending chase rather than a fulfilling journey. No amount of money is enough unless we have clearly defined priorities and lifestyle goals.

How do you want to wake up in the morning? This is a simple question, but your answer determines a lot. Once I figured out how I want to spend my days, I worked toward making that happen, rather than toward a financial goal.

WHO MAKES YOU HAPPY?

Think of the people who are important to you. Maybe it's a spouse, a child, a parent, or even a friend. Whom do you want to spend your precious time with? Time, after all, is a commodity. Knowing why we choose certain people over others is helpful in overcoming peer pressure. This kind of prioritization has always helped me know why I make certain sacrifices. I would much rather drive that 2003 Altima into the ground than pick up a huge car payment when I know that I get to take my kids to the park whenever I want. Maybe this decision allows me to plan a visit to Walt Disney World with my family, and that means more to me than the kind of car I drive. It is important to think not only about whom you want to spend your time with, but why.

Before I take on a new project or pursue a business idea with a friend, I measure my decision based on the time it will take rather than the money I will make. Some people think they have eighteen years with their kids, but I look at that time differently. I see twelve precious years during which my kids will live with us *and* want to spend time with the family. Once our kids reach their teenage years, it's hard to pry them from friends and the activities they enjoy. The days of holding their hand while crossing the street and going for spontaneous ice cream trips decrease in frequency. Sure, my kids love our kayak trips now, but how will they feel in five or ten years when all they can think about is the game they missed or the girlfriend they left behind? Is the money I'll make really worth the time I'm spending away from my kids?

TIME IS OUR GREATEST RETURN

Our time is finite. It is also the ultimate equalizer. Whether it's the checkout clerk at your local supermarket or Bill Gates, we all have the same twenty-four hours in a day. What if our daily schedule includes a two-hour commute, followed by a nine-hour workday, followed by two or three hours at home catching up on tasks for the next day? This routine is the reality for many of us five days a week. For some—those who love their job—it's a great reality. They find wealth in the happiness that their work brings them.

If our job does not bring us overwhelming happiness, it's time we look at our *time*. How are we spending it? How are we managing it? My definition of wealth is the ability to use my time the way I want to use it. Nothing on Earth is eternal. I want to spend my time with the people I love, doing what I love.

Everyone prefers to spend their time differently, so our definitions of wealth will vary drastically. If you love running your business and you wake up excited to take on the next challenge, a full, wealthy life most likely means spending your time at work. Perhaps happiness for you, however, is enjoying your cup of coffee every morning until ten o'clock. What decisions do you need to make to provide yourself with this kind of freedom? Ultimately, it all comes down to figuring out how we reclaim our time.

Controlling our time is our key to freedom. However, we must buy this key because it is not free. This is where the money part comes in.

Rejecting conventional finance and choosing our own clear path toward financial independence can be difficult. What are you gaining, though, when you make your own decisions that are not influenced by conventional standards and practices? I experienced a gratifying return on my time when I analyzed my spending and made sacrifices up front.

One of my biggest regrets is how I invested my time before I learned a difficult lesson. My dad moved in with us in Texas not long after he retired. He loved the little 1950s-themed diner in our city, and we discussed establishing a standing date at that diner every Friday morning for breakfast. Unfortunately, I waited. I wanted the kids to be older before I started this new weekly routine so that the two hours I spent with him on Fridays would not eat into my work time, and eventually into my time with the kids. I figured that when our youngest turned five, the whole family could go to breakfast and enjoy our time together in this new family tradition.

In theory, my plan was not a bad one. Sadly, however, my dad passed away eighteen months after moving in with us. Our tradition never got off the ground, simply because I thought I didn't have the time. I had the time; I just had to prioritize. It might be uncomfortable to take a three-year-old to breakfast, and work *is* important; but, had I realized time's fleeting nature, I would gladly have given my dad those two hours every week.

When we delay important things, "later" is not guaranteed. No other event in my life has made me so keenly aware of the value of time.

FIND YOUR PURPOSE...AND YOUR WEALTH

The best way to find your life's purpose is to think about the three things you want the important people in your life to say at your funeral. While this may sound morbid, it is the clearest way to see your life's purpose. What do you want your spouse to say, or your kids? Perhaps what your coworkers might say about your achievements comes to mind.

Despite who it is or what they say, it's important to write these three things down. Most wealthy people who provide advice—think Tony Robbins or Napoleon Hill—encourage followers to write, and to write frequently. Write down your objectives, your priorities, your goals, your ideas, and organize those thoughts. Making your subconscious both conscious and tangible is a great step toward finding happiness, fulfillment, and real wealth. Saying these thoughts aloud is also beneficial.

Simple activities like writing what you want people to say about you and visiting your local bookstore to see the aisles where you want to spend your day are helpful in finding your life's purpose. I know that I could spend hours in the finance and investing section of Barnes & Noble. In fact, that's how I spent my post-high-school days—it was clearly my calling. Now, I wake up every day and read about finance and economics for hours. This makes me happy, and I am able to make money and a successful career from following my passion.

Also, think about the work you would do for no payment, or about how you prefer to spend your Saturdays and Sundays. This is a way to qualify your time so that you can quantify it by making money. Many of us throw away what we enjoy doing because we think we have to choose a job based on money alone. We all need money, but why not enjoy making it? After all, we make more money when we enjoy *how* we make it.

PLAN AND PRIORITIZE

Just like a diet, you have to follow a plan to achieve real wealth. It's about making behavioral changes *and* shifting your mindset. Start by asking yourself how you want to spend your time, and whom you want to spend it with? Who and what do you value most in life? Your plan can be as simple as writing down your answers to these three questions. Check in with yourself every six months by revisiting your answers to ensure that your priorities are in line with the life you want. We all need an occasional reminder of the goals we've set and the reasons we've chosen our path.

Our idea of wealth may change throughout our life, and our plan should reflect those changes. To this day, when I think about wealth, I no longer think about money and financial wealth. It doesn't matter to me if I have $1 million or $10 million. What matters is if we have enough income to sustain our lifestyle. Our family's net worth and our monthly passive income statements do not excite or scare me. Instead, I ask myself, "Are we living the life we want to live?" As long as I can answer that we are, I'm happy.

CHAPTER TWO

WHAT DID WE INHERIT?

Money is not the goal. Money has no value. The value comes from the dreams money helps achieve.

—ROBERT KIYOSAKI

Millennials, according to generational researchers Neil Howe and William Strauss, were born between approximately 1982 and 2004. Despite our complicated reputation, I'm proud to be a millennial. We are environmentally conscious, and we appreciate the beauty of nature and the value of a sustainable lifestyle. No matter what side of the aisle we identify with, we believe that less petroleum consumption is necessary to preserve our future. I love the organic, farm-to-table, free-range mentality that millennials embrace, and I strongly connect with the ethical treatment of animals, even the ones we consume.

Millennials often get a bad rap—for being lazy, entitled, and unnecessarily frustrated. The media and older generations often talk about how millennials are not achieving what baby boomers did in their time; but those of us in the millennial generation are living with different options than the baby boomers had in their youth. Baby boomers could attend college while working a part-time job, and they could graduate debt free. Over the last decade, the government-induced inflation has made it nearly impossible for students to graduate without a mound of debt.

What's wrong with wanting to retire at fifty? What's wrong with knowing there has to be a better way to spend our lives than working day-in and day-out at jobs we detest? It's okay to want and demand more from life—even if others qualify that as lazy or entitled.

Change is hard for people to accept, especially when that change involves a mindset shift.

Millennials are purpose-driven people. We prefer to support small, local businesses rather than corporate giants, like Walmart. Activism is big in our generation, and we are quick to take a stand for what we believe in. Our problem is not that we expect too much; our problem is that our expectations are unprecedented.

THE MILLENNIAL STATE

The plan that our baby boomer parents passed down to us worked for them. It was possible to earn a college degree *and* apply it to a relevant career field. They could remain with the same employer for thirty years, earn a pension, and be commended for their company loyalty. Career fields did not change as quickly as they do today, and the economy was more stable.

By the time we joined the workforce after the 2008 market crash, the economy we heard about no longer existed. We found ourselves in jobs we did not want, with debt we could not control. As millennials, we have two huge problems we face as a generation: our nation's public debt and our college debt. The first problem is largely out of our hands. Past generations voted for an unsustainable government and borrowed prosperity to the detriment of the present day. Social Security is a resource that millennials and subsequent generations will not be able to access.

Our college debt, however, is possibly the biggest burden we face as millennials. Universities raised the price of tuition to astronomic levels, and the government funded school loans with no expectation of payment while we were in school. Basic economics tells us that if the cost of behavior is removed from the consumer, reckless spending and a volatile situation present themselves.

At eighteen, students borrow money for tuition with little thought to their post-college years. Sometimes, they are overly optimistic about how much money they will make when they enter the workforce; other times, they are naive to the reality of loan repayment. Universities aren't just businesses. They are *smart* businesses that charge their customers anything they want, knowing that the government will fund them. Once students graduate, they face a large amount of debt that is sometimes equivalent to a mortgage. The first years of adulthood look bleak for many millennials, especially considering the fact that only half of all college graduates are employed at a job that requires a college degree, according to *Forbes*. Perhaps, they have a degree in software, but they work as a bank teller—this is an all-too-common scenario.

Graduates also face a volatile employment situation because many employers are struggling with the various government mandates and employment regulations that have changed the employment landscape. Decades ago, employers used to be able to hire employees for a service with no strings attached. Now, depending on the type of employee, they are legally required to provide healthcare and worker's compensation. Retirement planning and company-matched funds may even be part of the employment package. From the employer perspective, employees are no longer a valid partner in the business.

The reciprocal impact is that the benefits many employees once experienced are becoming relics of the past. In the late 1970s, the 401(k) was introduced, followed by the IRA in the 1980s. Baby boomers were showered with new employment incentives and benefits when they first entered the workforce. As millennials, we are now on the other side of that. These programs and incentives have either crumbled, been drastically reduced, or been completely eliminated.

While many see this as a negative trend, I see it as positive. Thanks to the internet, many employers are hiring a new type of employee: the independent contractor. Technology has worked in our favor in this case, allowing for more freedom and independence with the freelance economy. Millennials, in particular, are taking advantage of it.

CHANGE IS NOT ALWAYS BAD

Being on the cutting edge of technology benefits millennials in many ways. We can, for instance, purchase stocks straight from our phone instead of setting up an appointment with a broker. We have countless investment choices, like crowdfunding, that were not options when baby boomers first started participating in the economy. We are a mobile generation, with the trend toward working from home only increasing in popularity.

Millennials talk about retiring at thirty or forty, but we're actually working a lot less in careers we love. I watched a recent TED talk in which a gentleman in his early thirties discussed how he enjoyed his job as a software engineer. He had held this position for years as he saved his money and lived frugally. Despite his happiness with his career choice, he decided to take a break—for a year he traveled throughout Indonesia, seeing and experiencing a new culture and lifestyle. When he returned, he was refreshed and motivated to start a different life. Instead of returning to his former employer—who had filled his position—he became a freelancer. He found ample job opportunities and increased independence, making more money than he had before.

If you want to be an entrepreneur, it's now easier than ever. Millennials, especially, are involved in new business ventures that did not exist ten years ago. The old way of thinking tells us that if we want to start a business, we need a building and a product; but people are writing profitable blogs, starting their own consulting services, and selling products direct to consumers by going to GoDaddy.com and purchasing a domain to start their own website. Companies like Facebook, Twitter, Instagram, Snapchat, and YouTube are now huge vehicles for blossoming businesses and new entrepreneurs. Entirely new markets are even emerging, such as the cryptocurrency market, where people are making a substantial income solely through investment.

Twenty years ago, creating a viable newsletter would have required the cost of paper, printing, and mailing fees on a weekly basis. Think of the time and expense this would impose upon a tiny startup. Today, I can do everything online without the need for a large warehouse to protect everyone's data, since I can easily use Google's resources. I am able to benefit from the infrastructure of a billion-dollar server with all of its features and security, and I don't have to pay a thing. Likewise, with a smartphone, tablet, or laptop, I can work from anywhere that has wireless, free of charge. Some technologically progressive cities, like Singapore, even have Wi-Fi running throughout the city.

With all the benefits of increased independence, technological advancement, and a chance for more prosperity, it's hard to look negatively at the millennial situation. The baby boomer plan worked for some, but even among the baby boomers who enjoyed home price appreciation and rising stock portfolios over the years, more than half of them have little more than $5,000 in retirement savings, according to the Economic Policy Institute.

Maybe the big difference between millennials and older generations is that we prioritize differently based on our circumstances. Many millennials, for instance, are forgoing home ownership and choosing to rent. I argue that the decision is not due to laziness, but rather to lending standards that are some of the strictest Americans have seen in the last forty years. Students who graduated in the 2000s and hit adulthood after the 2008 real estate crisis face a marketplace that demands a high credit score and a 20 percent down payment to purchase a home. Generation Xers—the generation between baby boomers and millennials—bought homes between 1998 and 2008 when interest rates were low and lending standards were lax. The playing field of home ownership is vastly different between millennials and other generations, greatly impacting our values, priorities, and purchasing decisions. Perhaps millennials are so difficult to understand because we create our own ideas of wealth, and we use our money differently. Home ownership may not be a priority, but the freedom to have coffee with a friend in the middle of the workday may be.

We still have many opportunities ahead of us as millennials living in the baby boomer aftermath. To capitalize on them, we need to let go of the old plan and its expired opportunities. We should redirect our energy toward embracing a simpler lifestyle that doesn't require three hours of commute time and nine at hours at work. It's easier now to complete our work on our terms with more free time—but we have to be willing to take chances, decrease our spending, and simplify.

EMBRACING CONCEPTS, NOT TRENDS

Some trends can be taken too far. As a financial expert, I appreciate the tenets of the millennial idea of minimalism that promote more responsible spending habits, but money remains an important tool that buys comfort and happiness. There's nothing wrong with wanting a home that's larger than one hundred square feet, or with preferring a nice hotel to a campground. When we stay true to our values and our definitions of wealth, it's easier to adopt progressive ideas.

While we reject some notions of the past in favor of sustainability and minimalism, some cultural values are difficult to shake, no matter the generation. Millennials are not immune to the appeal of luxury brands and the habit of overspending. In the past, someone in their mid-twenties might set their sights on a gold Rolex or an expensive sports car. Now, the sports car and watch are replaced by an iPhone and Tesla. Even the stocks of high-priced, well-established brands like Tiffany & Co. and Calvin Klein are currently near all-time highs. Luxury goes a long way in American society, no matter our age.

Sustainability is the key feature of the millennial mindset in which the value extends far beyond recycling and the tiny house trend. Our *lives* can become more sustainable by cutting spending and rethinking what we need. Everyone, no matter our generation, can be comfortable with a lot less.

In the next chapter, we'll discuss ways to eliminate this overspending that clutters, confuses, and ultimately buries us in burden and stress.

CHAPTER THREE

OVERSPENDING IS OUT

Remember the laugh we had when we traveled together to Hong Kong and decided to get lunch at McDonald's? You offered to pay, dug into your pocket, and pulled out ... coupons!

—BILL GATES TO WARREN BUFFETT IN HIS 2017 ANNUAL LETTER, "WARREN BUFFETT'S BEST INVESTMENT"

We don't typically think that the richest people in the world are thrifty. With all the money they want, why do they need to worry about the price of a Quarter Pounder? Most millionaires don't simply wake up wealthy one day. Through hard work, smart decision-making, and self-control when it comes to spending, they establish a healthy mindset about money that lays the groundwork for fortunes that are almost impossible to lose.

Controlling our spending, though, is easier said than done.

My wife and I have done things to save money that would make some people anxious. When our two dachshund dogs had rising medical bills, we gave them to a nice family. When our friend was letting his property go into foreclosure, we paid him a small monthly rent to squat on the property for nine months. This was in 2008, when the real estate market in Southern California collapsed— and when we started over. Sure, we could afford our dogs, and we didn't have to squat, but we knew it was time to make some tough decisions that would benefit us in the long run.

It was hard for us to leave Los Angeles and move to the desert, an hour away from our friends and family. We bought a 1,300-square-foot home for $95,000, knowing that we could pay that off in a few years and greatly reduce our overall debt and monthly bills. Leading up to that point, I felt shackled and overwhelmed. I didn't want to be poor, yet I didn't want my time and freedom taken from me in work obligations. I was prepared to make any sacrifices necessary so we could live the life we wanted.

WHO WANTS TO BE A MILLIONAIRE?

Michael Bloomberg is one of the most well-known billionaires in recent American history, with access to whatever he wants, most likely whenever he wants. Interestingly enough, Bloomberg owns just two pairs of shoes. One is a pair of sneakers for exercise; the other is a pair of dress shoes he has owned for ten years. He re-soles them when necessary.

This is not the type of behavior we normally equate with millionaires and billionaires. As a high school student in the late 1990s, I watched Puff Daddy and Mase flash diamonds and ride yachts in their music videos. To me, this is what it meant to be wealthy. I thought that everyone with a lot of money lived like a celebrity, without exclusion. In reality, celebrities experience an entirely different income level than most of us are capable of comprehending, based on their work, residuals, and endorsements.

In the book *The Millionaire Next Door: The Surprising Secrets of America's Wealthy*, Thomas J. Stanley and William D. Danko follow a group of millionaires throughout a twenty-year span, studying their income and behavior. From their research, we learn that the average millionaire almost never lives in a home worth more than $350,000 and drives a Ford Taurus. So, who is driving all of the luxury cars we see on the freeway? Most of them do not belong to millionaires. As a testament to this, BMW recently reported that 86 percent of luxury car drivers do not qualify for the millionaire bracket. This means that a large segment of society purchases luxury items disproportionate to their income level. The question is, do we want to look and act rich, or do we want to *be* rich?

Millionaires are frugal, price-conscious people. They save money and are not wasteful. In fact, the top 1 percent of income earners save 38 percent of their income, compared to the bottom 90 percent, who save just 4 percent, according to University of California, Berkeley economists Emmanuel Saez and Gabriel Zucman. Millionaires shop at Costco, and they go out of their way to find cheaper gas—even if that means driving a few more blocks and doing a U-turn to save ten cents a gallon. You will not find the average millionaire wearing a Rolex; they opt for sensible watches around $250 instead.

If you want to be a millionaire, mimic millionaires. I've learned from the countless financial books I've read, from Stanley and others. I not only changed how I looked at wealth, but also my exaggerated ideas of what a millionaire is really like.

I have interviewed at least four billionaires and more than one hundred millionaires, and amongst them, not one has inherited their money. Stanley cites nearly 90 percent of millionaires as being self-made. They are married, with kids, and they typically have jobs. Of the decamillionaires studied, almost all of them were business owners. This goes against the common belief that the wealthy inherit their riches. Perhaps we believe this because we can accept the idea that we do not have that kind of money despite all of our hard work for the simple fact that no one gave it to us.

It's also important to note that you don't have to own a business to become a millionaire. Most millionaires are regular W-2 employees. They haven't won the lottery or had a revolutionary idea, like Facebook. There's no silver bullet or luck involved—just hard work, smart decisions, and a higher than average rate of savings.

Interestingly, most millionaires spend little time thinking about their finances. Stanley and Danko found that once millionaires plan their strategies and budgets, they allocate only a small amount of time weekly, or even monthly, to focus on their financial activity and investments. They rarely move, living in their homes much longer than the three-year average of many middle-class Americans. When they *do* move, millionaires put down a sizeable down payment so that their mortgage accounts for less than one-third of the price of their home. Not only do millionaires stay in their houses longer, they stay in their marriages longer, too. Millionaires have a higher percentage of long-term marriages—not surprising considering that financial problems are the root of many divorces.

Clearly, we can learn a lot from millionaires. The most important feature of the millionaire mindset is their frugal nature. Being frugal does not have to mean being cheap—but we do have to be smart with our spending.

The middle class is currently in a reckless state of spending. Between daily Starbucks visits, financed BMWs, and a cultural habit of dining out, our spending is catching up with us. In *The Automatic Millionaire: A Powerful One-Step Plan to Live and Finish Rich*, author David Bach discusses "The Latte Factor," the phrase he coined for the money we spend—and lose—with all of our Starbucks trips. He did the simple math to demonstrate that spending four dollars a day, three hundred days a year for ten years, sets us back $12,000. While our daily lattes might bring us joy, what are we sacrificing for them? We may not get rich by saving four dollars a day, but we are establishing dangerous habits that spread into spending in other areas of our lives, as well. Our mindset toward spending—and overspending—has to change.

THE WEALTH DIVIDEND

The rewards of adopting a sustainable, frugal mindset extend far beyond financial. It actually feels good when we change destructive habits, even if those habits feel right in the moment. When I started making my own coffee at home every morning, I realized how much I enjoy the process. I enjoyed a better cup of coffee for less money, and I had the satisfaction of making it for myself. I get that same benefit from making our meals at home. When my family and I go to Chipotle for dinner, we spend an average of forty dollars for the entire family to eat. Sure, we have the benefit of a quick meal and no mess, but we could have made the exact same meal we eat at Chipotle for a fraction of the cost. Not only that, but we would have more time together as a family, doing something meaningful and constructive from which everyone would benefit.

This is a wealth dividend that many fail to consider when they buy meals to save time, and indulge in daily lattes. Again, what does wealth mean to you? What does it look like? If I buy a nice thirty-dollar bottle of wine, I can take it home and enjoy it in the backyard with my wife. We can take our time, avoid the taxes, cork fees, and noise of a restaurant, all while indulging in the same bottle of wine that would most likely cost twice as much to drink in a restaurant.

When our country is not at war, the government terms the money spent at home "the peace dividend." A wealth dividend works in a similar way. When we are happy and fulfilled, we do not spend our money according to corporate advertisements and high-end products. We reinvest in more income or save money, enjoying the idea that it is available. The *wealth dividend* is money available to use how we want, when we want, and it is the other types of wealth we discussed in Chapter One that have nothing to do with money. It's time with our loved ones, peace of mind, and a more enriched, meaningful life.

As Americans, we get caught between working and spending the money we make, without realizing the time and control we lose in the process. We don't have to spend money to enjoy ourselves, although we've been conditioned to think otherwise. A lot of my family's favorite activities, like spending a day at the river, catching crawdads and enjoying a picnic, cost nearly nothing; yet, we often remember these experiences more than the ones that come with a hefty price tag.

Once, on a trip to Panama, we met a family who was part of the Guna Indian tribe. They live a peaceful life, focused on their families, with few leaving their islands and joining the rat race of the outside world. Typically, they fish and take care of their daily responsibilities in the morning, and they return home to spend time together in the afternoon. Some sell products, like coconuts, on trips to Panama City, where they also purchase clothing and fresh water.

Some of the young Guna adults venture out and find employment outside the tribe. When they return, they tell stories of a completely different life—one in which people work all day without a break. Many prefer to return to the islands, and to the lifestyle to which they are accustomed.

Of course, this is an example of a completely different way of life, but we also see differences between our way of life and that of Europeans, as well. Go to Spain or Italy, and you find many stores and restaurants closed between two o'clock and four o'clock for an afternoon siesta that includes a nap, coffee, and tea, or simply some downtime to regroup. A slower way of life is built into their culture, even while keeping up with the demands of a fast-paced global economy.

THE SUSTAINABLE MINDSET

This type of awareness about how we spend and where our money goes is one of the first steps toward mimicking a millionaire and achieving financial independence. Millionaires are good at being frugal, but they are also good at using the things they buy for their full value.

Keeping our cars for as long as possible is sound financial behavior, but the middle class is notorious for changing cars every four or five years, destroying their wealth in the process. If we keep our cars less than five years, we should lease them instead. New cars depreciate in value the minute we drive them from the lot, and lengthy financing plans drain us for years. The same principle applies to home ownership versus home rental. Buying a home is expensive, with price volatility and the cost of upkeep. Also, what if we sell the home in three years and the value decreases 20 percent? Our money is gone in a short period of time—money that many of us lose easily because we fail to consider the expense of moving and home ownership.

Culturally, we're not accustomed to a sustainable mindset because we rely on financing everything. We might be approved for a $300,000 mortgage, but that doesn't mean we have to buy a home in that price range. A home closer to $200,000 is a more comfortable investment, but few of us will opt for the smaller house. Banks do not approve us for amounts that are responsible or comfortable. Instead, they stretch us as far as we can go with the least risk of default. In many cases, banks approve loans with payments equal to 55 percent of a lender's income. I've seen people who have no business spending more than $200 a month approved for a $900 monthly car payment.

At first, it can be hard to accept a less luxurious lifestyle, but after you know what you can achieve in just five years' time by focusing on sustainability and comfort rather than excess, it feels good to live within your means. Most importantly, you will begin to appreciate your new lifestyle.

We may feel that between our spending cuts and simpler, more frugal lifestyle, life is not as exciting as it was before. It's true—sacrifices and change require hard work and discipline, which are not glamorous. However, this is when we focus on the benefits we will see in every aspect of our lives within ten years. When we think of "financial plans," most of us conjure up a distant future forty years from now, when we can *finally* reap the benefits of our plan. I'm suggesting a different kind of strategy. By eliminating debt, cutting expenses, and buying our income, we can—and will—be financially independent within ten years. In fact, we will see major improvements within five years.

It's liberating to minimize expenses. One of the best feelings in the world is paying off a house, even if that house is smaller than the one you might have imagined for yourself. There's a time and a place for the bigger house and the fancy cars, but not until we achieve financial freedom.

THE OVERSPENDING EPIDEMIC

When I use the word "overspending," almost no one believes I'm talking about *their* spending habits. They don't drop $2,000 on concert tickets, so what I have to say does not apply to them.

Maybe you don't have a Lamborghini or a sprawling McMansion in a ritzy neighborhood, but I *am* talking to you. We all have our own interpretations of what it means to overspend, but our society has adopted a financed lifestyle that is the definition of overspending. Purchasing homes twenty times our annual income and financing vehicles worth half that amount is normal for Americans. It also is why we all are living in debt.

When a purchase is financed, that means we cannot afford whatever it is we are buying. It's difficult to accept, but it's true. I'm talking here about the money we borrow for consumption—for the expensive vacations, the houses, and the cars. Our credit card debt. Borrowing money to leverage investments or to fund a business opportunity that yields vital income is different from consumption debt.

The other caveat is that, admittedly, we all need shelter and transportation. It's completely normal and acceptable to finance a home, but I challenge the cultural norm of borrowing $500,000 for shelter. Financing $70,000 or $100,000 may not give us the house of our dreams, but it provides what we need at minimal debt, until we can truly afford more. Also, there's nothing wrong with renting until you save enough to decrease your mortgage to an acceptable, sustainable amount that can be paid off within a few years.

Our options for transportation are limitless, and, unless we live somewhere without public transportation, no one *needs* a car. It's a nice luxury item, however, and that is exactly the problem: its functional purpose of transportation has been replaced by what it means to us culturally, as a status symbol. No one *must* finance a car. We all can come up with between $2,000 and $5,000 for a used vehicle. While it's not exciting, and while we most likely will drive the worst car of all our friends, we will not have debt—and that is, quite literally, priceless.

WHY DO WE DO IT?

Overspending and indulgence have become part of the American tradition. Invite anyone from another country to experience a holiday in the United States, and they will be shocked at the excess food consumed in a single day. We eat a lot and we buy a lot because we think we *need* a lot. It's the American way and, to some extent, it has become part of our DNA.

Truthfully, it feels good to spend. Study after study shows us that spending money gives us the control we lack in our lives. Many decisions are made for us every day, from what time we wake up to what days we are allowed to relax with our loved ones. It makes sense that it's not only satisfying to shop, but also a relief on a subconscious level. We can buy what we want, when we want, and we are completely in charge of the decision. Introduce credit and our normalization of debt—another element of American culture—and now we have a vehicle for our cathartic spending, with few limitations.

As Americans, we have not always lived with this amount of acceptable debt. The introduction of the credit card made borrowed prosperity the norm and, suddenly, consumption was a definitive American trait. Today, we do not need to *be* prosperous to *feel* prosperous, as long as we qualify for a certain credit limit. Swipe the Visa and we have the luxury car, the nice clothes, and the fancy vacations. We pay for it in the long run, but the instant gratification that credit provides feels good—and it feels normal. Just look at our national debt to see how spending and borrowing have reached astronomical proportions.

So why do we do it? Why do we spend more money than we have, with little regard for the consequences down the road? For one, we learn from what we see. From the time we are young, we learn one thing about money and see something completely different in action. Our parents buy us piggy banks and talk about the importance of saving, yet they finance their TVs and make monthly payments that only cover the interest.

In a way, we have accepted our fate. We know there is no more Social Security and that we cannot rely strictly on 401(k)s to get us by in our golden years. If we have to work until we die, why not overspend now? Why not charge everything? With no map to guide us toward financial freedom, we will not be rich tomorrow, or even in five years, anyway. Just a $50 monthly payment covers our credit card obligations, and $800 per month is nothing for the car of our dreams. After all, we want to be like our friends. Whether we realize it or not, we feel pressure from the shows we watch on TV and from the wealthy neighbors down the street.

We stick together in this justified mentality of over-spending because it's comfortable. As a culture, we have a market of investors who spend because it's the norm. When the crowd buys nice houses and finances everything, when they have the neighbors over for big barbecues on Labor Day with their financed pools, it doesn't feel unnatural—even if they cannot afford it.

What is uncomfortable is being outside the crowd. When I pulled up to meet friends in my 1992 Toyota pickup in the early 2000s, the brake squeaking for a quarter of a mile and rust lining the fender, I was not proud that I looked like an idiot. I knew, however, that I was working toward something greater. By that time, I was already making money in real estate, and I was working hard toward financial independence. I had a plan, and delaying gratification was part of it. I knew that finding financial freedom meant I had to use my greatest freedom of all— my freedom of choice.

This is one of the best things we have going for us, as millennials. It's okay—and even great—to go against the norm and own our future. We no longer feel obligated to get married or have kids. We can work from home, buy our own benefits, and invest where we want, when we want.

It's easier and better than ever to follow our own path and make purposeful decisions that we *want* to make. The peer pressure that we face as millennials today is very different from the peer pressure felt by previous generations.

CUT IT OUT

The first steps toward financial freedom—and living like a real millionaire—are cutting expenses and creating a budget. Start by reviewing your bank and credit card statements to find out where your money goes. Circle or highlight the items that are not critical items you need. That might include clothing, meals at restaurants, or unnecessary Target runs.

Get rid of these unnecessary items because, after all, this is discretionary spending. Next, return to the list of items you need and begin cutting there. Can you reduce your electricity bill or your water consumption? There's always room to cut, even from the "need" column. Maybe you have an unnecessary extra refrigerator in the garage adding to your utility bill, or your air conditioning runs all day. When you begin the process of streamlining your consumption, you realize the amount of excess in your life.

Let's look at the variety of ways we can drop the extra baggage of expenses and responsibilities we carry around with us every month.

CONSUMPTION-CUTTING HACKS

- If your mortgage or rent is too high, you know the solution—it's time to move. Find a smaller property that allows you to save on utilities. Cutting back on housing expenses saves us the most in the long run. States like California, New York, and New Jersey are notorious for their high income taxes; Texas and Florida have no income tax (and they have warm weather, too).

- DirecTV is fun, but it's not necessary. If you know someone with DirecTV, you can ask them for their login and watch the shows you love the next day on your computer. You can do this with Netflix, as well—it allows up to three users.

- A gym membership feels like a good decision, but it's an expensive one. Think of all the extra money you spend as part of your gym routine, from the expensive shoes to the lunches at the chicken bowl place next door. Cancel the membership and walk to work if possible, or find exercise you can easily do at work or at home.

- Eating at restaurants is a pricey endeavor for a variety of reasons. The price of appetizers and dessert is often as much as an entrée, and any drinks you order bump up the bill considerably. If enjoying an alcoholic drink is important to you, make sure you factor that into the total cost of dinner, and look for other areas to cut back on the bill. You can also bring your own mini shooter and add it to your drink, or have a drink at home before or after dinner.

- Think about what you like to do for fun and look at the habitual, seemingly extemporaneous spending that happens every time you do that. For instance, when my family and I visit a theme park, the cost of admission is a major expense, but we also get ice cream every time we visit. If you're not ready to cut the special treats like theme park visits or an occasional nice dinner, consider cutting back on the extras that are often part of the experience.

- We seldom think of the costs associated with our job. We focus on what we make per hour, without deducting the cost of gasoline for driving to work, or the cost of lunch every day. It's important to look for ways to cut spending at work, too, whether that means packing a lunch or using mass transportation.

- Car insurance—and every type of insurance—is a big money pit. Consider raising your deductible from $500 to $1,000.

- Taxes are unavoidable, but you have some control over your monthly taxes and how they impact your income. Accept a smaller refund in April and increase your monthly income by claiming more dependents. After all, depriving yourself of your income for the sake of a higher refund is an interest-free loan to the government.

- Food is an easy place to cut expenses. Discount grocery stores sell "uglier" food at greatly reduced prices. Also, look at your spending at the grocery store. Typically, the most expensive items are the ones that can be eliminated, like alcohol, meat, and processed foods.

HERE'S YOUR CHANCE...ARE YOU READY?

Change starts by asking ourselves what we really need. Food and water are obviously important, as are housing and utilities; but what else is also essential? Sometimes, we are so busy paying the bills for unnecessary items that we don't have time for the type of reflection that will help us prioritize and organize.

What I'm offering you, with this book, is an opportunity to find your financial freedom within the next five to ten years. You will have to make serious sacrifices, swallow your pride, and do things that some people may find unacceptable. Maybe it's time to sell the house that you love but cannot afford; or maybe you need to change your diet and cut the expensive foods like meat. Don't simply live with your mistakes because it is uncomfortable to make changes or ruffle feathers. No doubt, some people, including your family, will question your actions. Despite what others think, and despite the initial discomfort of change, it's all worth it. In fact, it can even be fun once you find your stride and know that all your actions have a greater purpose.

You'll most likely cancel your gym memberships and shop at different stores. One of the hardest adjustments, however, is that the borrowed prosperity of your friends will seem more noticeable. They will continue driving expensive cars and enjoying lavish vacations, and you will have to accept this, knowing that you are working toward a greater good. After five years, once you have achieved your financial freedom, it will be *your* turn to pick up the tab at a nice restaurant with friends—and you won't have to put it on your credit card.

After five years, you may be able to quit your job or find another job that you enjoy, even if it does not pay a lot. You will be able to sleep in and travel the world with your family on extended vacations. I know this can happen for you because it happened for me. I chose not to attend college, and I did not have one particular skillset that pre-destined me for success that the average person cannot achieve. I worked hard to learn everything about finance; and, in some cases, I learned the hard way through my own failures. This is how I *know* that everyone is capable of making these simple changes. It just takes a mindset shift and determination.

In the next chapter, we'll discuss how these shifts impact our views on retirement, and what life holds for us at the end of the road.

CHAPTER FOUR

RETIREMENT IS NOT WHAT IT USED TO BE

You can want in one hand and crap in the other, and see which one fills up first.

—MY DAD

The day before he died, my dad went on an eighty-four-mile bike ride. Sadly, when he went riding with friends the next day, he suffered the heart attack that killed him.

He didn't have a pension plan, so he retired with just his 401(k). Not long after retiring, my dad moved into our guesthouse and lived a dream life. Every day, he woke up early and went for a bike ride, either on his road bike or mountain bike. He finally had time for his hobbies, and anyone who looked at his life would think everything was perfect. My dad had his bike, his grandkids, and Netflix. But if it rained for five days in a row, as it sometimes does in Texas, a bike ride is not in the cards. And it's easy to burn out when you are watching TV to fill your time. For all the freedom that he gained in retirement, my dad also lost a certain motivation and enjoyment for life that working had provided him.

For fifty-two years of my dad's life, he worked hard five days a week. During his twenties, he rode bulls; in his thirties, he began working at a mold injection company, where he remained for more than three decades. His role at the company was vital, and his responsibilities were specialized. When my dad discussed his intention to retire with management, they knew he would be hard to replace, so they offered him part-time employment. When he turned that down, they asked him to come in only eight hours a week. For my dad, who was raised with the mindset that you save for retirement, then collect when it's time, it was all-or-nothing: he was either working and saving or he was retired and playing.

My dad was retired for a total of eighteen months before he passed away. While he enjoyed his retirement, I often wonder if he would still be alive today if he had accepted his employer's part-time offer. With a different mindset about retirement, one that embraced a passive income portfolio, he could have achieved a balance throughout his life between the hard work that gave him meaning and the hobbies that he loved so much. He would not have worked hard with little downtime for most of his life, only to retire with all the time in the world and no direction or purpose to fill it.

It's healthy to work. Go to any tourist town in America, and I bet you will run into a retiree who is a tour guide or ticket collector. According to the Federal Reserve, one-third of retirees return to some form of employment, and half choose to remain working part-time. Sitting around and doing nothing all day may sound appealing when we are chained to a desk, but when we actually find ourselves without purpose, boredom becomes a heavy cross to bear.

What if we adopted a different mindset about retirement? What if we enjoyed our work but no longer depended on it for survival, either now or down the road? Finding financial freedom means letting go of our reliance on a 401(k) or on a pension plan. When we achieve financial independence, we clear our debt and we use passive income to pay the bills. Understanding real wealth enables us to prioritize where we spend our time. Achieving financial independence gives us the freedom to choose *how* we spend our time.

A STRESSFUL SITUATION

There's an old saying that the quickest way to death is retirement—an old adage based in fact. A study published in the *British Medical Journal* in 2005 analyzed Shell Oil retirees who quit work at fifty-five, sixty, and sixty-five. Researchers found that those who retired later in life actually lived longer. In fact, the retirees who quit at sixty had similar mortality rates as those who stopped working at sixty-five. Maybe our golden years aren't so golden when we make major life changes after thirty or forty years of routine and purpose.

When my father retired and moved in with my family at sixty-eight, he anticipated feeling nothing but free and happy. In reality, he spent the first six months being frustrated. I finally sat down with him and asked why he was angry and upset all the time. "Danny," he said, "I've worked most of my life, since I was sixteen. Now, I don't know what to do with myself. I have no responsibilities, and it makes me uncomfortable." Even if he still had purpose in his life, he lost something that was very meaningful to him.

Work can be healthy and something that people actually enjoy. Whether we are in corporate America or home raising kids, we thrive on routine and the fulfillment of doing good work and getting rewarded for it.

At nearly ninety, Warren Buffett gets up and works most days during the work week. His business partner, Charlie Munger, refuses to retire at ninety-five. Why should they? They are active, reasonably healthy, and they love what they do.

We know that early retirement doesn't guarantee us extra years, but why is it statistically so hard for us to handle? It's easy to understand when you imagine losing your career, income, healthcare, social life, and everything familiar to you every day. Your world is turned upside down, and it's supposed to be your pinnacle achievement. Just the thought of it is overwhelming and anxiety-provoking for many. Dealing with these kinds of changes is survivable if we are in our thirties; but the adjustment is difficult in our seventies. What if we slip and injure a hip? Or, God forbid, our working spouse suddenly passes away? The uncertainty of life, combined with a fixed income, causes anxiety for retirees at a time in life when their physical body can least handle it.

RETIREMENT'S COMPLICATED HISTORY

Retirement as we know it is a relatively new concept. The entire concept began as recently as the eighteenth century. Whereas there was once little hope of breaking away from the family trade, growing industry made it possible to consider professions outside of being a farmer or a blacksmith. We embraced notions like capitalism and individual liberty, and for the first time, financial wealth was skyrocketing. The quality of life around the globe greatly improved, and the idea that people might actually stop working and enjoy their later years became a wonderful reality.

Still, retirement was not a mainstream concept that everyone embraced and expected until the early part of the twentieth century. It was only when the German government began funding socialized retirement accounts in the wake of World War I that the idea of retirement went mainstream.

When our thirty-second president, Franklin D. Roosevelt, created Social Security as part of the New Deal during the Great Depression, Americans had their first government-funded safety net. It was a half-baked idea designed as a temporary solution to prevent the poorest of the poor who outlived their life expectancy from slipping through the cracks. For all that Social Security was—and is—it was *not* intended as a permanent fix or as a retirement fund. At the time of the New Deal, life expectancy was a meager sixty-two years of age; now, life expectancy in the United States is seventy-nine. FDR and his people thought that they had their bases covered by extending the program to those only over sixty-five, as arbitrary as this age was. Times changed, while distributions did not. Even today, our failing Social Security system is offered to those over sixty-five. Americans are outliving what was supposed to be a temporary financial solution offered to the select few who lived beyond their expected years—and they outlive it by fourteen years, on average.

After World War II, price controls were implemented in the United States. Employers needed a way to incentivize their employees, since they could no longer provide the wage increases they had relied on in the past. Suddenly employees were offered health benefits and retirement, normally through a sustainable pension program.

A pension is a guaranteed retirement plan offered by an employer, whether that employer is the government or a private company. While more sustainable than government pension plans because they are generally more conservative, the private pension has deteriorated over time. According to the Employee Benefit Research Institute, 67 percent of employees in the private sector with a retirement plan in 2008 only had a 401(k). The private pension, in other words, is becoming obsolete.

Government pensions, on the other hand, promise too much to recipients to stand the test of time. Many county and state pension plans are even bankrupt, as politicians have inflated pensions to appease voters. We all love our teachers, firemen, and police officers, but when a deputy sheriff works at a certain wage for thirty years and retires at the captain pay grade, he receives this escalated level of pay for the rest of his life. Instead, he should receive an accumulation of what was saved over his career to foster a plan that lasts. Life expectancy has increased, and the retirement of many government workers is longer than the number of years they worked.

As early as the 1970s, it was obvious that pension plans were not the solution. Employers began pulling back because they could no longer afford the pension system, forcing them to create the 401(k) and the IRA in the latter part of the decade. While the IRA is government sponsored, the 401(k) is an employer-sponsored retirement plan in which eligible employees contribute a percentage of their own salaries. Employers then choose whether they will match a certain amount.

The 401(k) and IRA had a good twenty-five-year bull market in which retirees in the late 1990s and early 2000s were riding high, but even these systems are showing signs of weakness. Imagine retiring in 2008, when the S&P went down 40 percent. What happens when we are supposed to withdraw 4 percent from our nest egg, but the market crashes? These plans offered hope for a permanent retirement program, but they were unfortunately not the solution, either.

Our government is still manipulating Social Security to give us the perception that it works. As bankrupt as it is, the Social Security system is doing significantly better than the government tells us because they have under-reported inflation. If we use the same methodology the government used in the 1980s to track inflation, Social Security checks should roughly be 100 percent more than they are today. According to John Williams, an economist and the founder of ShadowStats, a newsletter and website offering factual alternatives to government statistics, if we apply the government's 1980s methodology, we could estimate that senior citizens are currently losing 45 percent of their Social Security check. What does this mean for millennials? There will be nothing left of Social Security for millennials by the time they're seniors. If there are funds, they will be in the form of a small survival check rather than the government-sponsored retirement plan it has become.

Since the birth of the first retirement program, every succeeding system has been an experiment, whether Social Security, the pension system, or a private stock market retirement vehicle like the IRA or 401(k). Even more concerning, we have yet to see one full generation go through the current solution of the 401(k) and the IRA, and we are still shy of twenty years into the Roth programs. Each system morphs and adjusts, yet none of them have proven their sustainability.

THE BUSINESS OF RETIREMENT

Retirement often feels like an ancient system, especially when considering the countless rules involved. We are told we have to max out our 401(k), and that we should work as long as possible before we retire so we can experience the full benefits of Social Security. The problem with these rules is that there are a lot of unknowns, too, including life expectancy, the future of the stock market, and even the tax rate five years into the future.

Two things are certain when it comes to retirement: retirement has been a lucrative industry for Wall Street with all its fees and commission, and the majority of the general public has failed miserably at it. Research from financial groups like Fidelity and Bankrate tells us that 55 percent of the current baby boomers heading into their retirement years have retirement accounts that are grossly underfunded. In fact, according to the Insured Retirement Institute, 24 percent of baby boomers approaching retirement have nothing saved.

Financial advisors in the retirement business religiously follow the Four Percent Rule. In accordance with this rule, they advise their clients to establish a goal of retiring with twenty-five times the amount of their current income saved. The plan is to then withdraw 4 percent every year, adjusting for inflation, over thirty years. So, what happens if we live forty or fifty years past the age we retire? Also, anyone who has become adept at saving money knows how physically uncomfortable it can be to extract money from a savings account. Imagine establishing a system of aggressively saving money for forty years, and then, once you enter your later years, completely changing how you look at, save, and spend money. All of this happens at a time when most people are growing increasingly set in their ways and long for comfort over change.

Many retirees become extraordinarily frugal out of fear and uncertainty, although they own a house worth $500,000 and a sizeable pension plan. The Four Percent Plan and other retirement agendas sound nice when we read about our limited options in a financial planner's office at thirty. However, when we are seventy and quit our job, thus relinquishing the only source of income we've ever known, our retirement plan seems a lot less stable than we remembered it to be.

We have all experienced the discomforting feeling of withdrawing from the principal of our savings account. It's one thing to save for a vacation, then withdraw that savings when it's time to take the trip; it's something else completely when we have to take a chunk from savings for an unexpected expense, like a surgery or burst pipe. The essence of the retirement industry and its Four Percent Plan is based on the *requirement* to remove huge chunks of money that will never be replaced. It's an unnerving concept.

They say that nothing is certain except death and taxes, but tax rates are possibly the most unpredictable element of our nation's financial system. During World War I, taxes soared as high as 90 percent. Now, thanks to President Trump's tax cuts, Americans are paying fewer taxes than since before 1930.

Reduced tax rates, however, are not always beneficial for those relying on a tax-deferred savings system like an IRA. It doesn't help that the government is in collusion with the financial industry in a business model designed to convince us to give our money to Wall Street. Typically, we receive a tax reduction when we purchase stocks in an IRA or 401(k). But if we change our minds, we are assessed a 10 percent early withdrawal fee as punishment for taking our money back from Wall Street. In addition, the mutual fund industry is littered with fees. While the sticker may advertise a 2 percent fee, the amount is much higher in reality. According to a recent segment on *60 Minutes*, a 401(k) plan that advertised this 2 percent fee actually included seventeen different fees within the mutual fund. Over a thirty-year period, retirees relinquish 30 percent of their savings to Wall Street as the price to pay for managing their money.

A NEW WAY OF LOOKING AT RETIREMENT

Social Security is bankrupt, pension plans are on the

verge of bankruptcy, and we are finally growing out of the idea that the stock market is a reliable place for our retirement dollars. Our idea of retirement has not evolved with us, failing to deliver the financial security and fulfillment we thought it would.

Instead of thinking about how much money we should save, perhaps we should approach retirement first by asking ourselves if the career we have chosen is how we want to spend our lives. Are we doing what we love to do, and are we putting money toward the people and the things that matter most? As millennials, we are good at reflection and self-introspection—let's use this ability to figure out *when* we want to work, *how* we want to work, and *why* we want to work.

Once you set financial independence as your goal, you will never look at retirement the same way again. After all, being financially independent means that you can technically "retire" in your thirties or forties because you no longer need active income to pay your bills. We followed the retirement age of sixty-five because of Social Security, but now the rules have changed. In fact, there are no rules. If we want to quit working because our passive income is paying the bills, nothing is stopping us. We may find that we have no desire to retire, but having the ability to make this decision, especially before we hit sixty-five, is the definition of financial independence and real wealth.

In place of conventional retirement and the Four Percent Rule, we should focus on capturing passive income. We don't have to withdraw from a pile of cash we've saved for three or four decades when we're making passive income because our principal investment stays intact. Invest in income, whether it's a single-family rental property, a private real estate investment trust, or a crowdfunding investment in which you receive a return on your loan. Make the dollars that you have saved create new dollars, then use that income to pay your bills.

Nothing is better than getting paid for a job that you enjoy. Regardless, with financial independence, passive income should pay the bills, and active income should be a bonus. Next, let's talk about how we can make passive income a present reality and a long-term solution to replace retirement.

CHAPTER FIVE

PASSIVE INCOME PAYS THE BILLS... NOW AND IN THE FUTURE

Never depend on a single income. Make investment to create a second source.

—WARREN BUFFETT

Upon purchasing my first duplex at eighteen, suddenly I was making $600 a month. That's a huge monthly dividend for a beginning investor. The $600 covered my car payment and my insurance, and I still had a few hundred dollars left over to cover other expenses. I saw passive income as a viable solution for a wealthy lifestyle—and I was completely addicted.

The secret I learned then is what I want to share with you now. Whether you're daunted by the impossibility of retirement or you're feeling like your time and life are not your own, the answer is the same: passive income is the key to your financial freedom, now and later.

WHAT IS PASSIVE INCOME?

Passive income is the money we make from an investment or enterprise in which we are not actively involved every day. It can be a yield earned from a funded loan, or an investment idea that requires more time and commitment, such as a rental property. It's the potential income your dollars can earn, with little effort from you. Once you make the decision to put it to work, your money brings in additional money, enabling you to spend your time exactly as you want.

Passive income breeds a healthy mindset because we decrease the uncertainties that a changing economy can throw at us. I use passive income to cover all my bills, from our food and electricity, to our groceries and dinners out. If something happened to my business—to my active income—my bills would be covered and my lifestyle would only slightly change. Relying on active income to cover all my bills would create a catastrophic situation if I lost my business.

A sense of peace, prosperity, and independence come from passive income—this is precisely why it's the most lucrative way to build wealth. Losing a job, closing a business, or taking time off are catastrophic when we rely on active income alone, but with passive income, we create options for ourselves. Whatever happens, we can sleep peacefully at night, knowing that our lifestyle is entirely covered by our investments.

It's never too early to think about ways to build passive income. We can start focusing on ways to invest in our teenage years or early twenties. Income compounds itself, and ten years passes quickly. Before we know it, we have a passive income portfolio of $500 or $1,000 a month, rooted in a minimal income invested when we were twenty. Making money early in our adult years allows us to save more; combine this with smart spending, and life is off to a great start.

If you are thirty or even forty and you make an average income, you can start investing for the first time and become financially independent in five to ten years. The equation is simple: cut expenses, become debt free, and invest in new strategies for passive income, like rental real estate properties and crowdfunding, in which your investment is one of many in the financing of anything from mortgages to oil tankers. This frees your time for what you want to focus on, whether that's a job that makes active income or increased time with loved ones. However you decide to spend your time, passive income enables you to abandon your reliance on retirement and enjoy your life now.

One of the best feelings is paying monthly bills with passive income. It may start gradually—an electric bill covered one month and a grocery trip covered the next—but when your money starts to compound, the benefit becomes clear. Passive income can buy you time, which, as we've discussed, is invaluable. Life is good when you have enough extra income to pay for a special family vacation, or when you make an extra $15,000 one year that allows you to take extra time off work. The numbers don't have to be large to start making a difference in your lifestyle and overall feeling of wealth.

BUILDING PASSIVE INCOME

You can start building passive income with only twenty-five dollars—this will not bring you a large return at first, but it's a start. Lending Club allows you to begin crowd-funding investments with them for this amount, and even investing with great publicly traded companies like Budweiser or Disney—if you buy at the right time—can yield a good dividend from a minimal starting amount. The most important thing is that you start investing, and that you set financial goals as you consider your investment options.

Consider some quick numbers. With a $5,000 investment, it's possible to make fifty dollars a month. Can you imagine making an extra fifty dollars each month for the rest of your life? That money might cover your cell phone bill, or maybe even an electricity bill if you live in a small house. You could even use that money to buy more income. It's easy to see how all our mandatory monthly expenses could be covered with smart investments. A traditional financial advisor might tell you to put that $5,000 into an IRA or some other retirement account. In thirty years, you may make money, but depending on the economy, you may be left with nothing. Earning passive income is an achievable feat, and we don't need a million dollars or a finance degree.

It's hard to imagine, but with no debt, most people can live off $30,000 a year. It may not be the ideal lifestyle, but it's doable. As we've discussed, most people have hefty car payments and mortgages to cover, which makes living off passive income alone more difficult. Remember, though, that nothing mandates we live a certain way. It's okay to want to rent instead of buy a home, just like it's okay to decide against having kids or getting married. We can build the life that *we* want, despite what the government and advertising or family and friends may tell us. This is why it's also okay to decide that working for active income is not for us, and to decide that passive income alone is the way to build our future.

WHAT ARE YOUR OPTIONS?

Entering the world of investment for passive income is exciting. It can be overwhelming, too, if you don't know where to begin. Let's look at all the opportunities available to you, and why some may be a better fit for you than others.

CROWDFUNDING

Crowdfunding began when Lending Club first pooled smaller investors together to fund personal loans for customers. Today, crowdfunding is no longer an exclusive investment opportunity for the rich, and its accessibility is increasing its popularity in the investment world. In fact, crowdfunding is becoming so popular that it has the potential to rival the banking industry.

With crowdfunding websites like PeerStreet.com, investors come together to act as the bank for home mortgages. This can be an appealing investment option because mortgages are generally some of the safest and most stable investments.

When we look at how banks and insurance companies invest, we notice that they purchase many first trust deeds, or first liens on properties. Banks never buy the homes; they fund the mortgages behind the homes, meaning that this asset belongs to the bank until the owner pays off the mortgage. This type of investment is almost always 30 percent down, if not more. This means that when we invest in crowdfunding, we are part of the pool of investors funding the mortgage on someone's home. It's better to be in the position of the bank than in the position of the landlord—we collect mortgage interest payments monthly, but we have none of the issues associated with tenants and rentals.

The benefit of crowdfunding, in addition to returns of anywhere from 7 to 12 percent, is that the amount of equity in crowdfunding largely protects against the limited risk involved. Technically, as with any other investment, we could still lose all our money. However, the team behind recommended crowdfunding companies is composed of smart people who have stress-tested their portfolios for every market in which they participate. They research, and they provide examples of what might happen if prices dropped in a particular market similar to the situation in the 2008 housing crisis. While an event like this is rare, occurring only once every fifty to one hundred years, it provides investors with peace of mind to know that someone is assessing their risk. In the event of a foreclosure, the company can foreclose on the property, sell it, then repay the investors, sometimes even with a profit.

Any time we invest our money, we should look at the people behind the operation. You have to trust who you work with, and you want to know if they have a serious team handling your money, or if they are simply a small shop with no reputation.

PeerStreet

PeerStreet is one of my preferred crowdfunding options because of the people behind it. One of the seed investors is Dr. Michael Burry. If his name sounds familiar, it is most likely because Christian Bale recently played him in the movie about the 2008 housing bubble crisis, *The Big Short*. Also, founder Brett Crosby, in addition to starting PeerStreet, founded the company that eventually became Google Analytics.

PeerStreet allows investors to diversify their investment amongst different mortgages. Whether you invest the minimum of $1,000 or $15,000, you are crowdfunding the mortgages of others with hundreds of other investors.

When I spoke with Brett Crosby, he talked about how PeerStreet disrupted the mortgage industry to the point that they have become indispensable to the basic loan companies that originate the loans. In some cases, if a loan defaults, the loan originator might fund it because they don't want to lose their good credit with PeerStreet. After all, PeerStreet handles a large number of mortgages that large banks like Wells Fargo, Bank of America, and JP Morgan cannot accommodate.

Let's say that you sold a house and you are purchasing your next home. You need a bridge loan, more colloquially known as a "house flipper loan," because your house closes in sixty days, but the new house closes in thirty days. In the past, bridge loans were localized per their respective market—then came the internet revolution. PeerStreet decided to expand the local markets for crowdfunding, enabling investors in Los Angeles to fund loans in Atlanta, for example. Local banks, small-group investors, and individual investors were no longer the only options for loans.

Now, PeerStreet is the go-to company for bridge loans. You call PeerStreet, show them the deal, and before long, an appraiser evaluates the property and obtains a broker's price opinion. A title search is completed, and PeerStreet does everything necessary to ensure that the equity of the property aligns with investment preference. They get 1 percent of the deal. This means that with an interest rate of 9 percent, investors get 8 percent.

Lending Club

Let's use Lending Club as another example of how crowdfunding works. Most of us are familiar with Lending Club as a resource for loans and consolidating credit card debt. Obtaining a loan from Lending Club requires a credit score of 675, with a job history of more than two years, and a household income of more than $75,000 per year.

These qualifications allow investors to fund the loans with peace of mind, knowing that borrowers have good credit and stable jobs. As I mentioned, the minimum to begin investing with Lending Club is twenty-five dollars, which makes it a great place to start crowdfunding. The yield is anywhere from 5 percent to 15 percent, based on the level of risk you assume from the borrowers you select. Perhaps you only want to back those with a FICO score of 700, or an "A" credit rating. Despite a lower return of around 5 percent, once you build confidence, it becomes easier to take risks that yield 16 percent.

The tricky part of Lending Club is that their loans are unbacked. This means that if someone defaults on a loan, your only reprieve is taking the defaulted party to collections and threatening to ruin their credit score; otherwise, the borrowed money is gone. While Lending Club will handle the process of taking defaulted clients to collections, the money lost is partly yours.

Contrast this to PeerStreet. They have the same high-quality borrowers and a similar setup, but if the borrower defaults on their loan, they can actually lose their home.

In this case, PeerStreet will take over the home and sell it themselves. This added insurance makes investing with PeerStreet feel more secure, as long as you have more money to invest up front.

REAL ESTATE INVESTMENT TRUSTS

Real estate investment trusts, or REITs, work similarly to crowdfunding. With REITs, the government has allowed companies to establish themselves as real estate investment trusts as long as the companies distribute the majority of the income earned to the investor base. Investors receive their returns as dividends, rather than as business partners, cutting tax amounts and making REITs a more profitable investment option.

REITs are public or private, although I prefer the private option. If you've heard of publicly traded REITs in the stock market, these are the same thing. Private REITs have less liquidity, so they are not volatile like publicly traded REITs that are repriced every day on the public market. If you want to own a great business or a portfolio of houses, but you also want peace of mind, private REITs are the way to go.

I use several companies to purchase private REITs. These are companies that use investor cash to make sizeable purchases on apartment buildings, blocks of single-family homes, or commercial property. These are all investment areas that most people—including myself—would not choose to invest in directly because of the expertise required. Chairmen of these largest publicly traded REITs know how to invest in skyscrapers, for instance, *and* they run crowdfunding sites that enable the public to invest based on the chairman's knowledge.

While new to the general public, this type of investment has been around for a hundred years through Wall Street institutions like Goldman Sachs. When the US Securities and Exchange Commission approved additional crowdfunding options in 2012, everyone finally had the opportunity to participate. While it has been less than ten years since approval, crowdfunding has proven itself as a solid, safe investment option for the average American.

For private REITs, I use Fundrise, RealtyMogul, and Rich Uncles. All these sites work the same, but I diversify my investments because there is always risk involved with everything, and anything can happen at any time—think Enron or Bernie Madoff. This is why it's important that your money is spread around in different investments. All these companies are run by fallible people, so if something happens, no single event can run the risk of having a devastating impact on your future.

These private REITs yield anywhere from 7 percent

to 11 percent. Some of these companies issue loans as payment, and some pay outright cash. We want to look for a high yield and the type of income we receive from our contribution. This is an automatic, passive process—another reason to love it. The money I earn from these investments is directly deposited into my checking account every month. I suggest that you don't allow the money to compound, or to produce additional income on the principal investment. I'm not against compounding, but it's important to reallocate the money to another passive income investment, or spend it. Remember, you ultimately want to achieve the mindset that your income and savings can and *should* be spent.

It's easy to hoard money like a squirrel once you start earning it, but remember that this process is about changing your mindset. We are hardwired to spend active income only, as if the money we make when we exchange our time and hard work is expendable, but our passive income is not. Save your active income; spend the passive. It is important that we change this mindset because we must learn to trust the passive income, not fear it. Many of us see passive income as unstable, or risky, but it's just as stable as active income. After all, we can lose our job or close a business, and we no longer have that source of income. With very little risk associated with our passive income options, in many ways it's safer to rely on our investment earnings over time, especially as the returns build. Would you rather trust your financial security with an employer whose decisions are controlled by company profitability, or with your own safe, sound investment decisions?

REAL ESTATE

One of the best assets you can own is residential real estate. A single-family home is wonderful. Even better, purchase a multifamily investment, like a duplex or fourplex. If you are willing, it's lucrative to live in one unit and rent the others. While living with my dad in my early twenties to save money, I purchased three single-family homes and collected on the rent. Of course, it didn't take long for my dad to start charging *me* rent, and I decided to purchase a fourth house and move out on my own.

Purchasing real estate for investment is not complicated. The most important thing to remember is that you must buy at the right price. That way, the tenants' rent payments cover all the expenses *and* provide extra cash flow, even if it is only one hundred dollars per month. Many fall into the trap of buying real estate with hopes that it will increase in value. It's important to remember that real estate is a sizeable investment. If the numbers are negative from the initial purchase, it is nearly impossible to build wealth, at least for many years.

If you are new to the real estate world, it's a good idea to learn about purchasing real estate by picking up a book, reviewing YouTube videos, or asking a friend who has been through the process to coffee. *Real Estate Investing for Dummies* is a great place to start, as is Gary Keller's *The Millionaire Real Estate Investor*. Keller is the founder of Keller Williams Realty, and he provides valuable investment advice for the price of his book. You don't want to depend on a realtor or loan officer, both of whom work off commission and only want to close the deal—you need to protect your best interests.

When we have money to invest and are ready to build passive income, it can be difficult to select the right investment option because there are many. If you want the minimal amount of work, the crowdfunding option is your best option. However, if you have the time and you are willing to apply the effort necessary to purchase real estate at the right price, real estate investment will be worth your while. It's important to also remember that real estate investments require a financial cushion. Be prepared for an instance in which you cannot find a tenant, or a bad tenant has to be evicted. Remember that taxes, insurance, and mortgage must all be covered, whether or not you have a tenant. This is why it's vital to purchase properties in which we easily gain cash flow.

Working with a Realtor

In addition to property managers, I work with several different realtors in the markets that interest me. When I'm ready to buy a property, I contact these realtors and let them know my criteria. From there, I let them call me. I always vet realtors by making sure they made it through the 2008 housing crisis. If they did, then I know they can handle anything.

Consider shopping in different states, and even in different countries. I use websites like jasonhartman.com and the Marshall Reddick Network to connect with realtors from all over the country, which allows me to own properties in states I have never visited. I simply hire an attorney for the title and escrow work. The attorney's realtor, who is trusted and established, assists with the property purchase.

Start Small

Start small with real estate. Purchase condos first, or lower-priced single-family homes in your area. Keeping the situation sustainable in the beginning allows you to avoid situations with mounting bills, zero profit, and maximum stress. I've completed many real estate deals in the $100,000 to $300,000 range, and they have always been smooth and successful. The handful of deals I've closed in the million-dollar range have been painful because the numbers are bigger and more ominous. When something goes wrong in these situations, it is a problem that costs at least $20,000—at that rate, it's easy to lose control quickly.

If you live in a home that costs $500,000, do not purchase rentals in the same price range. Most likely, you have already purchased the maximum you can afford. This is when the homes or condos that cost $100,000 or $200,000 can return positive income immediately, as long as the rent covers all the associated expenses.

Shopping for the Right Investment

I buy houses with foundation problems, or homes that have serious fire damage. These categories of homes are my specialty, since I accidentally discovered that they are easier to fix than most people believe. Everyone has a different set of criteria for the real estate in which they want to invest, based on where they live and the opportunities available to them. Maybe they are buying in Tennessee and looking for a property that has a 20 percent return on rent, relative to the price. They might be buying in California, and want a fixer-upper or a probate property.

Fifteen years ago, I had an opportunity with a house in California that had a foundation problem. I immediately turned it down because I only wanted to focus on the paint, carpet, and blinds, like most real estate investors. Once we moved to Texas and I was forced to fix a foundation issue in our home, I discovered that the total cost was no more than $5,500. This is, without a doubt, the most intimidating home repair possible, yet even this major change costs so little. Typically, foundation repairs are between $1,500 and $3,500.

Also, it's easy to negotiate a reasonable price for the home, since most investors avoid houses with foundation problems, and banks will never loan on such a property. I would much rather negotiate on my terms with little competition than enter a bidding race against fifteen other buyers for a home priced below market value. In this scenario, chances are that I will end up buying close to market value anyway, just to compete with other investors.

Finance Your Investment

The next step in real estate investment is thinking about how to finance the investment. You might pay cash, or come up with a down payment using a conventional mortgage. You might also look for a seller-financed deal. In the last ten years, I have used seller-financed deals to purchase homes, rather than a bank loan or straight cash. Baby boomers are opting for seller-financed deals more often, as well. In these arrangements, the home seller owns the property free and clear. They list the property, noting that they want a certain percentage down, or a particular amount of money or term agreement. Perhaps they want 8 percent for ten years with a balloon payment in which the buyer pays off or refinances the entire house by the tenth year, or maybe they want 5 percent for fifteen years. Whatever the seller offers, the buyer can counter. This is the only pocket of the free market left. Once both parties agree on the terms and rates, payments are made directly to the seller instead of to a bank. The seller no longer owns the title—that is transferred to the buyer. Now, they simply own a lien on their previous residence.

When prospecting for a real estate investment, focus on the homes that pay you every month—these are the homes in which you can make a profit from the rent because the rent is more than the mortgage, the insurance, and the property taxes. To do this, hone in on regions of the country where you can make money from cash flow, like Alabama, Tennessee, Louisiana, Texas, and Florida. Markets in Las Vegas, Phoenix, and throughout California are difficult to obtain cash flow because these areas have seen a lot of appreciation. You never want to invest for appreciation because this simply makes you a speculator in housing.

Currently, there are contractions in the real estate market. We are in the end of the real estate cycle, where some home prices are declining in high-priced markets like New York and San Francisco. In the beginning and middle of the cycle, we can buy real estate from coast to coast and receive cash flow. Now, that cash flow is unobtainable—and impossible—in the higher-priced markets where home prices have reached their peak and are starting to slide.

Regions in the South and Midwest tend to be optimal because, in addition to providing cash flow, home prices do not rise and fall as drastically as in other, more desirable, regions. If we look at a housing chart in Las Vegas, for example, it looks more like a stock investment than real estate. California also closely resembles the S&P 500 when there is a big crash followed by a decisive incline.

The national crash of 2008 and the crash at the start of the Great Depression were both tied to the mortgage market. In 2008, specifically, when interest rates increased, the no-income, no-documentation loans blew up. Currently, people are maxed out with interest rates, foreshadowing another real estate crash in the imminent future. Lending standards have improved and banks are more liquid, but even these facts cannot prevent a crash. If interest rates normalize, we will see a serious correction in the hotter markets like California and New York.

Property Management

In the beginning, it makes sense to want immediate returns. In this case, managing your own properties is a good idea; later on, you can hire a property manager. I managed my own properties in the past, and I typically went months between problems that required my attention. It's not uncommon to hear horror stories about landlords fixing toilets at midnight, but those are exaggerations from naysayers. If, for instance, someone has an issue with a sink, I Google plumbers local to the property, and provide them with the tenant's phone number so they can coordinate an appointment. It's quick and simple, and it's rarely expensive. Working with property managers when you have the resources and multiple properties is convenient, since they handle the property inspection, credit checks, and rent collection.

For me, the most difficult part of property management was coordinating the signing of the initial rental agreement. If you want to manage your own properties and skip overseeing this step, you may retain a realtor who will charge anywhere from 50 to 100 percent of the first month's rent to handle the initial agreement process. They consult the MLS, or Multiple Listing Service, which provides all the past details about the property that only realtors can access. The more details you know about a property, the easier it is to negotiate a fair rental price and manage it. After reviewing the MLS, the realtor runs the applicant's credit score and customizes a template contract from the National Board of Realtors. Basically, they hand you the tenant.

In addition to property management, some people let their fear of evictions stand in the way of purchasing rental properties. It's not as intimidating a process as it may seem. Normally, we hire an attorney for anywhere between $300 and $1,300, depending on the state. Lawyers handle the entire process, from posting the sign on the door giving a three-day notice to pay or quit, to coordinating a physical eviction with the sheriff's department if the tenant refuses to pay or leave. In the twenty years I've owned rental properties, including the twenty-three tenants who are now leasing from me, I've only had to evict four parties. Renters typically feel comfortable enough to notify me if they are going to be short on their rent, or if they simply cannot afford it any longer. I work with my tenants as much as possible, because ultimately, it's easier and less costly for everyone involved to be reasonable.

I try to overdeliver as a landlord, mimicking the protocol of a Marriott or Hilton hotel. Don't think like a single-property landlord, think like a hotel CEO. Fix problems immediately and with a smile. Your tenants are your valued customers. One problem can easily breed another, if not handled positively and appropriately.

Collect Dividends

When we buy a rental property, not only are we able to write off the mortgage interest as a homeowner could, but we may also write off the real estate taxes and any improvements we make to the property. Anything from replacing the roof to managing the property from a home office can be written off in taxes. Always consult your CPA about specific tax incentives when you invest; with real estate, however, the incentives are almost limitless.

In fact, every year we may write off the depreciation of the physical house on the land itself, even when we are not actually losing money. The house may increase in value by $10,000 in the year, but that value has nothing to do with the wear and tear of the physical structure— the depreciation. This is the value that can be written off in taxes.

One of my favorite aspects of real estate investment is the leverage we have when we invest. If we want to buy stock worth $100,000, we need to come up with this full amount. As the stock market rises 10 percent, we make $10,000 and now have $110,000. Apply this to a single-family home investment. If we buy a house worth $100,000, we will probably need $10,000 for a down payment. If our house increases in value by 10 percent, it is now worth $110,000; but, if we look at our actual return on capital because of the leverage, we realize that we had a 100 percent return in one year from the $10,000 we initially invested as the down payment. This is because there is an easily available permanent mortgage market where we can leverage loans of various term lengths. If we come up with $10,000, we can control an asset of $100,000. This is great when we consider appreciation, but this is typically not the reason for our investment—we invest in real estate because we can collect a great dividend.

MAKE A BREAK FOR IT

Passive income is the way to achieve financial freedom, and crowdfunding and real estate are great options for making your investments work for you in both the short and long term. It's a safe, smart way to make money in a way that eliminates your dependency on an active income lifestyle. With passive income investments, you're in control.

The farther we get from the Wall Street investment mentality, as we will discuss, the closer we are to a sustainable lifestyle. In the next chapter, I'll discuss other investment options, in addition to crowdfunding and real estate, that yield profitable returns and keep us away from the volatility of the Street.

CHAPTER SIX

INVESTING BEYOND WALL STREET

An investment in knowledge pays the best interest.

—BENJAMIN FRANKLIN

In 2008, Warren Buffett bet any hedge fund that if they beat the S&P 500 over a ten-year period, he would donate $1 million to the charity of their choice. Likewise, if anyone accepted the bet and lost, they would donate $1 million to the charity of *his* choice. The only hedge fund that took him up on it, Protégé Partners, ultimately donated to Girls Incorporated of Omaha, the charity of Buffett's choice.

Whether you are the greatest investor in the world or just an average guy, studies show that beating the stock market is nearly impossible. If you happen to successfully beat the odds one year, you should cherish your moment of glory, since lightning rarely strikes twice. Even Warren Buffett has failed to beat the S&P 500 with Berkshire Hathaway, his own holding company, in the last ten years.

The entire financial industry is built on making us think that "it" can happen for us—that we can get rich from Wall Street. Think about it. Why do we hire financial advisors? Why do we pay them sometimes extravagant fees for giving us what we think is an edge? Why do we buy books, audio tapes, and newsletter subscriptions about the stock market? The financial industry is built on this hope that we can beat Wall Street.

When we start investing in publicly traded stocks, we assume a serious risk. It's like gambling in Vegas, except it requires a lot more time and money. The truth is, most of the money made in the stock market is made by those who work in the financial industry.

Every worker in the financial world applies a fee, makes a commission, or profits in some way by creating vehicles for us to "beat" the S&P 500. Brokers, for instance, make money off the trading commissions and the fees we pay when we trade in mutual funds. Goldman Sachs and Merrill Lynch, two of the world's largest investment banks, make their money from building mortgage-backed securities to sell to the world's pension fund. When they take a company like Facebook public, their payoff is huge. This is where all the money is made on Wall Street.

Wall Street is ultimately a wealth transfer vehicle. Like everyone else, I have lost money in stocks; I also have made a lot of money in stocks. The times I have "won," I have not been in the retail space, where people typically buy in the open market. I've been on the insider's part of Wall Street, purchasing stocks a year before their initial public offering, or IPO, because of my contacts and strategic positioning with the company. Brokers also invest in these early, pre-IPO rounds before a stock is made public, but rather than giving their clients access to these low stock prices, they scoop them up for themselves, then call their clients.

Holding stocks will not make you serious money. However, the brokers are making money on your hopes and dreams. The retirement industry, for instance, now trades on Wall Street, adding money into 401(k)s the first and fifteenth of every month. Their retail traders are instructed to buy but not sell. Wall Street, however, *is* selling, capitalizing on the volume that everyone provides them with on the first and fifteenth. Brokers sell retirement stocks, gaining liquidity and earning a huge commission.

While Wall Street sells us stocks, retirement programs,

IRAs, and annuities, traders and the companies behind the stocks never hold huge positions in these assets or vehicles. Instead, they hold cash.

Most of us will see the biggest return on our money *and* time by avoiding the stock market. We live in an era with countless options, from the straightforward options like crowdfunding and real estate investments we discussed in the previous chapter, to precious metals and whole life insurance policies that are rarely considered as viable investment options. It's an exciting time for everyone to invest, but especially for those, like millennials, who are able to embrace this new mindset early in life in such a way that it can truly impact their future wealth.

Keep in mind that there is no magical formula for asset allocation with investments. Some investing professionals, like Tony Robbins and Ray Dalio, subscribe to models that incorporate a retirement plan. Others emphasize diversification. I believe in mimicking Warren Buffett's philosophy that sticks with safer investments and less diversification. I also focus on the areas where I see others experiencing success, and I follow my own interests and expertise. For this reason, my personal asset allocation is roughly 60 percent real estate investments, 20 percent in businesses and the stock market, and the remaining 20 percent in alternative investments, like the oil and gas industry and precious metals.

My one standing rule in asset allocation is to minimize risky investments that rarely yield big returns. In other words, I stay away from Wall Street as much as possible.

STAYING OFF THE STREET

So if Wall Street isn't the answer, what is? It's time to undo the conditioning that has taught us to focus on speculation when it comes to our investments. When we buy stocks, we don't invest with an eye on the monthly dividends we will receive. Instead, we pray the stock prices drastically increase over time. It's the ultimate gamble.

The good news is that there are plenty of other investment options beyond Wall Street. In this chapter, we'll take a look at what some of those alternatives are.

MICRO-CAP MARKET

Micro-cap companies are publicly traded startups or established companies that have decided to go public. They have a lower capitalization—or stock, debt, and profit total—than large-cap companies. While it is important to keep in mind that 90 percent of our investment efforts should focus on producing more income than what is possible with the micro-cap companies, they are a great place to invest when you believe in the potential of a burgeoning industry and the people behind it.

Startups are inherently a riskier investment because of their volatility. For this reason, it's smart to have no more than 10 percent of your investable net worth in micro-caps.

Despite their risk, one of the things I appreciate most about investing in micro-cap companies is that it's a fun experience. As these businesses form and create value for themselves, they also create value for others. This is where true wealth creation comes from, and I like to have a hand in this process. I have almost no chance of meeting Disney's CEO, but I can meet the CEO of a micro-cap cannabis company and be part of creating this wealth. Investing in five to ten micro-cap companies is not a huge risk; maybe some of them go bust, while others have a mediocre performance. One might take off, however, and the investment return is anywhere from 1,000 to 5,000 percent—sometimes even higher.

There are two options for investment: buying on the open market or participating in a private placement. With private placements, investors provide companies with money to cover the cost of entering the public market, even though they may not go public for six months, or even a year. You must be an accredited investor with an annual profit of $250,000 in the last year, or a million-dollar net worth, to invest in private placements. With no liquidity in the beginning, investments cannot be immediately sold. Part of the benefit of investing with private placements is that investors are rewarded with cheaper shares, or a lower valuation of the company.

The open market is when trading begins on the company's stocks. Anybody can purchase the stocks by simply going through their brokerage account, whether that's Scottrade, E*Trade, TD Ameritrade, or any other brokerage firm.

The cannabis industry currently offers some great examples of micro-cap companies that are having their moment in the spotlight. Whether they manufacture edibles or vape pens, or are working on a patent for drink infusions, there is opportunity for the public to invest in these companies in their infancy.

We will never again see an end of prohibition like the one we are seeing right now in the United States. The legalization of cannabis has created a ten-year bull market for cannabis investors, not to mention a once-in-a-lifetime opportunity. In micro-cap investments like this, the people behind the operation are of utmost importance and prospective investors must take these players into account *before* investing. An idea may be great and a company might appear to have potential, but the people behind the company have to be credible, serious, and dedicated. If a terrible CEO assumed control of a large-cap company like Coca-Cola, no one would worry about bankruptcy because these companies are well established and nearly indestructible. Micro-cap businesses, on the other hand, are vulnerable to major change, especially when the leadership is questionable. Their entire success rides on the best and brightest leading them into the future.

I work with some CEOs who founded the companies they lead, and they don't collect a salary. Others receive a paycheck, but they dedicate their entire salary to the purchase of more stock on the open market. You should only invest in companies in which the management owns 10 to 50 percent of the company, thus demonstrating they have skin in the game. I only invest in companies with this type of leadership, because I know they are there to see the company succeed—not for the money or to make a name for themselves. I feel even better when CEOs have been featured in *Entrepreneur* magazine, or when they have been awarded top honors because they have demonstrated a notable level of success.

One of my favorite people to work with in the mining space is Keith Neumeyer. Keith has built two separate billion-dollar mining companies and is now working on his third. It's extraordinarily difficult to build a successful mining company, let alone one that garners $1 billion. Keith has done it twice.

Future Money Trends makes it our mission to identify and shine the spotlight on people like Keith. We look for the unicorns of the industry. Just like there are thousands of hedge fund managers and asset managers, there is only one Warren Buffett. Amongst all the giants in the tech industry, there was only one Steve Jobs. This is who we try to identify.

If I'm going to buy gold stock, I only partner with people who have successfully built a gold company. Although the cannabis space is new, I still try to find people who have built a successful company in another industry before entering the cannabis business.

PRECIOUS METALS

Ray Dalio, one of the most successful fund managers of all time, once said that if you don't own gold, you don't understand economics. In the last five hundred years, gold is the only asset that has never gone to zero.

Most financial managers tell us that 10 percent of our wealth should be stored in precious metals. While most of us don't do this, precious metals remain a significant asset that is often underestimated. I look at gold as insurance against the unknown elements of the financial industry. I do not own gold with hopes that it will increase in value. I own gold and hope it *does not* increase because if it does, that means the economy has taken a downturn. As a father of three, I would prefer Disney to increase to $10,000 a share and gold stay flat, or even decrease a little.

Historically, gold has kept pace with real inflation. Since 2000, gold has consistently beat the S&P 500, although comparing precious metals to the stock market is like comparing apples and oranges, since metals do not provide a yield. Gold also is not a business. It does not have press releases, or a management team who can screw it up. It's just gold, and it's true money. One hundred years ago, a gold coin, worth twenty dollars, might buy a suit. Today, twenty dollars might buy a pair of socks for that suit, but that same gold coin is now worth $1,300. There is no need for gold to make us money because it *is* money.

The only thing anyone expects from gold is for it to hold its value. It's smart to put anywhere from 5 to 10 percent of our investable assets into some type of precious metal, ideally gold and silver. If something unforeseeable occurs, we have our metals to fall back on.

If gold is true money, silver is its little brother. We can find silver in our cars, computers, licenses, and passports. Everyone who owns a smartphone even has about forty-five cents worth of silver. Its demand is going to continue to grow because of its shortage—whereas all the gold ever mined is still with us, most of our silver is in landfills because it's too costly to recycle it. For those deciding between an investment of gold or silver, choose silver. Not only is it rarer than gold above ground, it's more affordable, too, requiring eighty-four ounces to purchase just one ounce of gold.

Precious metals are inconvenient to sell, a fact that oddly enough increases their stability in comparison with cash. With a checking and savings account, we can simply transfer cash from one to the other and spend it. With stocks, we can click our mouse, and within a second, dissolve all our hard work and huge business asset into cash. Having too much cash is not as good as it sounds. After all, our dollar is not real money. It's a fiat currency, or a paper, government-backed currency that is not tied to anything tangible, or a specific commodity. The government can print as much as it wants, and the government is capable of making huge mistakes.

Fiat currencies have existed in three thousand different forms throughout history, yet not a single one has survived except for the fiat currencies we have today. It's quite possible that the dollar hasn't had a long enough history to expire, especially considering that 99.9 percent of currencies throughout time have ultimately dwindled to a value of zero. The dollar of Zimbabwe, for instance, used to have a one-to-one value with our own dollar. Now, it's worthless. This is why precious metals are so important, for now *and* for the future.

There are a few ways to purchase precious metals. The first method, through the stock market, is not a recommended strategy. Remember that one of the major benefits of gold is its sustainability in an unknown crisis. Would you want your most secure asset in the hands of a system subject to unpredictability? In the event of a major hack of the New York Stock Exchange or Merrill Lynch, where the majority of stocks are stored, precious metals purchased within the system are just as susceptible as the other stocks.

The whole point of owning gold is to remove money from the banking system. It's best to purchase it physically, through Miles Franklin or another precious metals vendor. These vendors will actually deliver the gold to you—you can hold it in your hands, and store it yourself. If you use Miles Franklin, they might store it for you in Canada, although you can also store it with offshore companies like Global Gold Corporation. I recommend storing gold on your property, as well as in a neighboring country and overseas. It may sound paranoid, but governments have a history of wealth confiscation. While many people are afraid of interacting with foreign governments, I find that our biggest threats come from the politicians close to us.

In the 1930s, Franklin Roosevelt confiscated gold from the safe deposit boxes of American citizens. This may not happen again in the United States, but I prefer to keep my gold out of our banking system. After all, which gold is more easily confiscated? The gold buried in your backyard, the gold stored with Brinks through a private company in Canada, or the gold that is part of the Enterprise Capital Fund sitting in JP Morgan's vaults? Our country is not immune to hard times, and it makes sense to seize the most control you can over a universal currency, like gold.

CRYPTOCURRENCY

When I first heard about Bitcoin, it was worth a dollar. In 2017, it was worth $20,000.

The purpose of Bitcoin continues to evolve. It's a cryptocurrency, meaning that there is no physical coin, nor is there a company we can contact. The golden coins with which we are familiar are simply marketing tools. It's a private currency, backed by a network of computers all over the world. Every transaction is open source on the blockchain, making the process unhackable. The blockchain tracks all activity from the first transaction. Each time the blockchain has a new transaction, whether from the single investor in their home office, or the large institutions in Iceland, it is instantly recorded and updated in the entire blockchain network. If someone wanted to hack Bitcoin, they would need to change the blockchain by hacking all participating computers around the world, while also figuring out how to travel back in time to alter the blockchain. Even if a hacker figured out a methodology for this, many investors store their Bitcoin in cold storage, where it sits separate from the internet on a USB drive in a safe or other secure, discrete location. Bitcoin is essentially impossible to hack.

Similarly to gold, Bitcoin is also a good way to store wealth. Our ability to upload our Bitcoin to a USB drive makes it possible for no one else to know it exists on the blockchain. Also, user names are replaced with numbers and letters for Bitcoin transactions, enabling another level of privacy.

Bitcoin has eliminated the middleman from making money. Most of us are so accustomed to dealing with a third party in transactions that we have forgotten that middleman even exists. When we transfer money, the bank, Western Union, or PayPal charges a fee—they make money from our exchange. The original point of Bitcoin was to eliminate not only the middleman, but also the trillions of dollars of banking fees and the potential risks of government-managed fiat currency.

While I suggest that roughly 2 percent of our financial

portfolios should be in the cryptocurrency sector, no one knows what the future holds for Bitcoin. At one point, we all had AOL accounts, and we used Yahoo! to search online; MySpace was our site for social networking. While I cannot say whether Bitcoin is a trend that will prevail, cryptocurrency currently is the only decentralized investment option. If hackers want to disrupt the stock market, they hack the New York Stock Exchange. If they want to target the national treasury, they focus on the United States Treasury Department. Cryptocurrency, on the other hand, is so decentralized that it's virtually everywhere. It's a safe wealth transfer process, and it's easier for international business. Since the Patriot Act was passed in 2001, foreign business transactions have become increasingly difficult—cryptocurrency remedies this fact. We can now transfer ten dollars or ten million dollars to someone in China without anyone, except the sender or recipient, knowing about the transaction.

From the government's perspective, cryptocurrency is not ideal. It's undeniable that it opens doors for illegal activity. However, think about the amount of criminal activity that occurs with US currency every day. I believe that having the opportunity to use a currency criminally does not make the currency inherently bad. There's nothing wrong with wanting to avoid banking fees or to conduct business privately. There is no need for me to tell Chase, Bank of America, or even the United States government that I'm doing something—my business is my business. Unless we are willing to abandon our sovereignty, our money is ours.

This decentralization is one aspect that separates Bitcoin from other cryptocurrency options. Unlike Litecoin, the longest-standing cryptocurrency behind Bitcoin, and Dash, which specializes in cryptocurrency as a payment and transaction option, Bitcoin has no founder or managing party. It simply began from a group of enthusiasts who understood the cryptocurrency technology and recognized its potential. Once up and running, these enthusiasts released Bitcoin and enabled it to flourish, independent of their guidance or structure.

As with any investment, it's smart to learn more about cryptocurrency if this is your first time investing in it. You can go to FutureMoneyTrends.com/bitcoin and download our Bitcoin reports, or you can learn more from Coinbase. Set up an account and familiarize yourself with the currency by starting with small transactions, perhaps just for purchases.

Bitcoin is becoming increasingly mainstream, and adoption rates are rising among both millennials and businesses. Whether Republican or Democrat, no one likes the idea of major corporations telling us who gets to make money. We've seen social networking sites, PayPal, and even Google deny people from using their systems. Bitcoin will never do that because no one owns it. It's not managed or controlled, and it's an open-source cryptocurrency. It's our way through bureaucracy, proving itself as more than just an investment trend, but a sustainable option for the future.

WHOLE LIFE INSURANCE POLICIES

One of my favorite options for passive income outside of investments is whole life insurance, considered one of the greatest investment vehicles for the rich. Forget the name because it's not term life insurance. This is cash value, whole life insurance from privately held mutual insurance companies that pays dividends. I use whole life insurance as a vehicle for savings and passive income, since purchasing it provides legal benefits from the IRS, through a lobby specifically for widows and orphans.

When we buy these policies, we act as a partner with the insurance companies. They perform their role, calculating the odds of particular events and forecasting, as policy holders benefit by sharing their profits. As you save with a whole life insurance vehicle, the cash value grows, tax-deferred. The company is required to take 90 percent of their profit and distribute it to the policy holders in the form of a tax-free dividend. We don't lose money; in fact, we are guaranteed to make money because we share in the profits of the safest industry on the planet. What other business takes money from customers but potentially never has to provide a service to them?

Whole life policies are known as the "Rich Man's Roth." We can only invest $5,500 a year in a Roth IRA. In a self-employed IRA, the cap is $56,000. With whole life policies, however, we can invest multiple times our annual income, with the same effect as the Roth IRA. They have roughly a 5 percent, tax-free yield that makes it seem like 7 percent. This is cash that is set to the side, lawsuit-proof, and usable any time it's needed. This is why it's a great vehicle for the rich—they can shelter millions of dollars from taxes with these policies.

Also, whole life policies are dual compounding, which means the cash value that grows at 5 percent can also be used as collateral for a policy loan, theoretically enabling us to purchase something else that yields an additional return. Let's say that your whole life policy yields $100,000 in cash value. As it grows 5 percent, you can borrow the $100,000 cash and invest it elsewhere. If you decide to invest in a high-yielding crowdfunding option like Fundrise, you can make an additional 10 percent on this original $100,000 investment. You still owe the insurance company their 5 percent annual interest, decreasing your 10 percent yield with Fundrise to 5 percent. Still, this series of transactions allows you to simultaneously make 5 percent with your original whole life policy investment, and another 5 percent with Fundrise. This is the dual compounding beauty of whole life policies.

I'm such a strong believer in whole life insurance that I have sixteen policies myself. When you think about, this is where the world's pension funds go for a safe return. In fact, the insurance business is what made Warren Buffett wealthy. He owns many companies, but Geico is his crown jewel.

If you are interested in learning more about this type of passive income, I recommend consulting Paradigm Life, a financial education firm that handles these policies, or the *Bank on Yourself* books and strategy by Pamela Yellen. It took me years to learn and understand how whole life insurance can act as a savings vehicle, but the educational process is worth the time.

TIME TO STRATEGIZE

We live in an era of lower-risk, higher-yielding investment options, as long as we know where to look. If you feel overwhelmed, visit FutureMoneyTrends.com for more information. For more information about becoming a cannabis investor, you can visit my investor's guide at FutureMoneyTrends.com/greenprofits.

While we may start investing with less money than ever before, we still need a source of active income to get the ball rolling. Fortunately, it's possible to make active income on our own terms now. In the next chapter, we'll discuss how the freelance economy is changing how we look at our time *and* our careers.

CHAPTER SEVEN

THE FREELANCE ECONOMY

The gig economy is empowerment. This new business paradigm empowers individuals to better shape their own destiny and leverage their existing assets to their benefit.

—JOHN MCAFEE

We were taught in school that once we were hired into corporate America, it was time to work our way up the proverbial ladder. However, the freelance economy changed how we think about our careers. In the freelance economy, the idea of a traditional job and the traditional corporate climb is gone.

Other names for the freelance economy might be the gig economy or the independent contractor economy, but unlike the independent contractors of thirty years ago, today's contractors do not necessarily perform a physical job like painters, plumbers, or electricians. Today, independent contractors also work from home by leveraging technology to build their own business.

At one point, work-from-home professionals were mainly transcriptionists and people who sent mailers. Of course, this has changed. Thanks to the internet, the freelance economy is unlike anything we have seen before. It has created a flexible economy—an economy perfect for millennials who like mobility and minimalism.

A FLEXIBLE WORK SCHEDULE

Some people call it the part-time economy; others call it the gig economy. However you refer to it, the freelance economy gives us freedom. We conduct business when we want, with whomever we want, and in whatever business sector we want. We can be a transcriptionist on Monday, an editor on Tuesday, and an Uber driver on Wednesday. We can have multiple schedules *and* multiple gigs, all with maximum flexibility.

In a freelance economy, we can design our own lives. If you want to spend the first hours of your day lounging around, drinking coffee, and going to a nice lunch, you can do that. If you wake up feeling sick, you don't have to call in to anyone. Starting your day at three in the afternoon is an acceptable option because you are your own boss.

Freelancers sometimes battle the negative connotations that come with this kind of independence. After all, it's not *that* job—the one with the 401(k), the pension plan, and the health insurance. The freelance career is about embracing a different life. The career you choose can be financially lucrative, fulfilling, *and* flexible as a freelancer. Flexibility is a powerful word—it's a powerful state of being. Being flexible allows you to unlock the very definition of wealth. Rich people have money, and the truly wealthy people use that money as a tool to buy time, the real signifier of wealth.

On a recent ride home from the airport, I realized that my Uber driver embodied this sense of wealth. He and his family are from Morocco, and he was thrilled to be able to work at night once he moved to the United States. He explained that he drives for Uber all night, then spends mornings with his daughter. He gets her ready for school, walks her there, then returns home to sleep in the afternoons. By the time she comes home, he's awake and ready to take her to softball practice. After tucking her in at night, he jumps in his car, drives to the airport, and starts his workday. It's a perfect life that makes him happy because he spends his time where it counts—with the people who mean the most to him.

I was impressed that he leveraged the freelance economy's flexibility and freedom to build a wealthy life for himself and for his family. Think about his daughter's perspective: she sleeps while he works, and when she needs him, he's there in body and mind. He's happy, present, and passionate about his life and about how he spends his time. If he finds himself in a situation where he needs more money—like for holidays or unanticipated expenses—then he can work more hours or choose to work on a Friday or Saturday night when the pay is higher. It's about *his* choices, and his ability to make those choices.

HEALTHCARE AND "RETIREMENT" IN THE FREELANCE ECONOMY

Possibly the best aspect of the freelance economy is that its flexibility allows us to live a semi-retired lifestyle. The biggest benefit retirees gain is extra control over both their life and time. This is exactly what the freelance economy puts back in our hands.

However, with this early sovereignty comes added responsibility. All this requires is a simple change in mindset. You will have to cover your own healthcare, and you will have to manage your own savings and retirement plan; also consider the fact that these benefits are figured into your salary when you are employed by someone else. As an employee, you might receive a monthly check of $3,500. In reality, this amount should be $4,500, but your company subtracts your healthcare and retirement because they "provide" these benefits. While it feels like your employer is giving you something for free, these benefits are actually deducted from your paycheck. On your own, you may find a better healthcare deal than your employer. As we've discussed, the 401(k) is really money for Wall Street.

It's important to figure out how you would manage your own healthcare and a smart savings plan now, whether you are an employee or part of the freelance market. Over the last forty years, we've seen a drastic decrease in the number of pensions offered to employees, especially in the private business world. Many of the healthcare benefits that employees select are also decreasing in value. I prefer to pay for my healthcare because then I can choose the coverage I want. We once selected traditional healthcare, but after the Affordable Care Act, our prices doubled. Now, we use a nonprofit organization. We pay $450 a month for our family of five. We are responsible for the first $450 of our monthly expenses, but after that, the nonprofit covers any overage. It works the same as our car insurance—we don't have insurance for oil changes and maintenance, we have insurance for unforeseen expenses. We may pay for doctor's visits, but we ultimately save money.

If I were employed and my employer covered my healthcare, insurance would be close to $1,000 for our family. Insurance would cover our doctor visits, but I would rather pay for doctor visits and cut my insurance payment in half. For those who are young and healthy, it certainly pays to buy your own healthcare.

If you are able to establish a bank account, you already have all of the skills necessary to set up your own IRA or 401(k). Also, being your own boss or a business owner gives you access to better retirement accounts than employees. As an employee who receives a 401(k) for work benefits, you select a fund from approximately ten different options, and you are assigned an account manager who can provide advice. However, if you own your own business, you can set up a solo 401(k) or a solo IRA and choose whichever fund you want. You can buy real estate, rental properties, gold, stocks, or private real estate investment trusts. Suddenly, all options are open to you. Not only is it more cost effective to be your own boss, but you also have increased opportunities.

Most of the tax benefits written into our tax laws in the United States are developed for the wealthy; the wealthy normally own businesses or have some sort of financial stake in them. This might not seem fair, but it's the way our system works, and we have to figure out how to maximize our resources.

HOW THE FREELANCE ECONOMY BENEFITS EMPLOYERS

There are many benefits to becoming a freelancer. Our cell phone becomes our business phone and is tax deductible. Cars and mileage are tax deductible when used for business, as is our home office, whether we rent or own. Businesses even receive incentives when we choose to become our own boss and work for them as a freelance employee or independent contractor.

Employees are a liability for companies, both big and small. As we've discussed, businesses are responsible for healthcare, retirement, and unemployment insurance. The minute you become an independent contractor, companies lose these three costly obligations. In some states, companies cannot fire an inadequate employee who is performing below standards. Every company, regardless of how many employees it has, must have documentation for everything, from the first interview to the exit interview. The red tape is exhausting for businesses, especially when options exist to work with contractors, minus the documentation and expense.

Imagine being a hiring manager and interviewing someone who wants the whole employment package—the pension, the healthcare, and the severance package. Now, imagine a freelancer interviews for the same job. They will perform the job at the same level of quality without any of the responsibilities that come with an employee. If they *don't* do a good job, you can fire them without consequence. There's no documentation, or 401(k) to establish, or even an email or office space to arrange. They simply do the work and receive payment, and you have a completed job.

It's easy to look at employers as the bad guys, with all the layoffs and program cuts employees have experienced throughout the years, but times are tough for them, too. I have a friend who is a business owner with eighty employees. He was recently forced to lay off twenty-five of them and decided to release an entire department. Women, men, black, white—everyone in that department was laid off. My friend did not anticipate issues of discrimination or unfair treatment, but one of the employees was three months pregnant. She filed a lawsuit against him, alleging that she was terminated because she was pregnant. Although everyone knew that was not true, the lawsuit still had the potential to cost my friend hundreds of thousands of dollars. Ultimately, he was lucky that his insurance company settled the case for him. For many business owners, the people they hire are their biggest risk.

I know someone else who owns a brokerage company. He hires full-time attorneys just to ensure that his business complies with regulations. Every time he hires someone or decides to open an office in another state, he has to weigh the associated risks and expenses with the benefit of the office. Every time he crosses a state border, there are even more regulations, headaches, and millions of dollars spent on attorney fees.

Kelly Services, the largest temporary employment agency in the United States, is now the nation's third-largest employer. The fact that a temp agency has grown to these proportions shows how employment is trending, and culturally, how we make money differently. It's about more than just money, though. It shows how we view our independence and time, too.

CAREER OPTIONS FOR FREELANCERS

Becoming a freelance employee is not about choosing an "easier" path or about sacrificing career options. It's about discovering what we love to do and making it work for us, on our terms. It's about wanting to work, and finding our sovereignty and independence. Best of all, most careers translate into the freelance economy.

THE INDEPENDENT CONTRACTOR

Amazon provides countless opportunities for freelance work, from using its affiliate program to sell products and advertising on a blog, to providing the opportunity for self-published books. Some steer clear of Amazon because of its potential to track consumers through Alexa, or because of what its resources are doing to the retail business. However, certain societal developments are beyond our control, and it's beneficial to figure out how to work with those developments, whether they represent true progress or not.

Almost the entire staff of FutureMoneyTrends.com is composed of freelance workers. From bookkeepers to copywriters, editors to personal assistants, they work for us because we provide them with ample opportunity for consistent work. They check emails, respond to subscriber inquiries, create advertiser invoices, and schedule podcast bookings.

Even my personal assistant is a freelancer. She was previously employed as a teacher, but similar to my wife, once she had children my assistant realized she never saw them during daytime hours. She worked all day, spent time in her car for her commute to school and back, and she even worked at night, preparing lessons for the next day. Now, as an assistant with FutureMoneyTrends.com, she has increased flexibility so she can spend time doing what she wants, in addition to her work. She walks her oldest child to school in the mornings, and she's home with her youngest throughout the day. Occasionally, she meets her husband for lunch.

In the past, a personal assistant's (or secretary's) day was much different. They often had to commute to the city to handle their secretarial duties, which mandated that they stay close to their desks. Most of us experience dead time throughout the day. We may be productive for a few hours, but many of the remaining hours are spent talking with other employees, having coffee, or perhaps attending to personal matters online.

At the end of the day, we all have a production capacity, and everyone organizes their time differently. It's not beneficial to employees or employers to chain people to their desk for eight hours a day. In the freelance world, the wasted time becomes *our* time. We can make better use of it—and employers don't have to pay us for it, either.

BLOGS AND PODCASTS

It's easy to find freelance work when we follow our passion. Maybe you like photography or videography, or maybe writing is either a hobby or a way to earn a living for you. There are countless blogs, magazines, and various media outlets looking for content. I once filmed five beautiful, brand-new homes being destroyed in Los Angeles when a construction project was canceled in 2008. Rather than pay the daily fines they received from the city, the project financers bulldozed the homes. I posted the footage on my YouTube channel, and before long, the *Wall Street Journal* contacted me, interested in purchasing the rights to the footage. They received new content, and I received a check for $500.

Podcasts are also a great opportunity for anyone interested in starting a business. It's best to find a niche, rather than try an all-encompassing subject for a podcast that has most likely already been done. There are already countless people who interview celebrities or successful entrepreneurs, simply to share their story. Finding something specific to discuss, on the other hand, not only increases audience numbers because your material speaks to them more clearly, but it also enables more effective and lucrative affiliate marketing.

Let's say that you discuss the flu on your podcast. Who are your listeners? Most likely, they are people who have the flu or want to prevent it, or they work in healthcare and deal with it on a regular basis. Regardless, the chance of this audience engaging with the podcast marketers on some level is highly likely, whether by purchasing a product or inquiring for more information.

Podcasts can be about anything, as long as they are specific. Podcasts about wedding planning in the fall, caring for a dog, or raising an eight-year-old boy are all good options because advertisers know who your audience is, and they will pay you to reach them.

SOMETHING FOR EVERYONE

Almost any job can turn into a freelance opportunity. Most pet sitters are freelance workers, and many nannies also work for themselves. House cleaning, home improvement work, and technology repair are all lucrative areas for freelancers.

There are many new industries to consider as a freelancer. Uber is a great example of a business that has experienced tremendous success from hiring drivers who work when they want, with their own vehicle, driving passengers to their destinations. There are other business opportunities in which you can rent your vehicle to someone. Also, consider Airbnb and other similar services. You can make money by renting your real estate property, as well.

IS IT WORTH THE RISK?

We assume that being employed is safer than freelancing; however, in today's environment of high expenses, liability, advancing technology, and globalization, employment is not the fail-safe choice it once was. Just because we are good employees does not mean we always keep our jobs, especially if we make a lot of money or if there is a cheaper alternative available. Now, it is riskier than ever to be an employee because of government regulations that have made them a burden to employers. We see self-serve kiosks and other forms of artificial intelligence in place of human representatives with startling frequency.

This does not mean that freelance work is completely safe. After all, with increased sovereignty comes increased responsibility. As our own boss, we are only accountable to ourselves. That may sound good, but when it's up to us to get out of bed in the morning, we need discipline and self-regulation to make money and be successful. If an Uber driver sleeps through the busy hours of work, they will never make the money they need to survive. If a nanny cannot get to work on time, the job will be gone before any sort of real income is earned. Increased independence might not be for everyone; but, then again, self-management and motivation are universal values for success, no matter the industry or environment.

For millennials, restoring individual sovereignty is important. This does not translate as laziness or entitlement. It means that we want to make our own path, separate from the path of our baby boomer parents—and that's a good thing. Our path may not be better, but it will most likely be right for us. The world today is different from the world of the baby boomers' younger days. It's only natural that different generations have different lifestyles, and that they expect different things. Consider someone who turned eighteen in the 1980s. The United States was the dominant global power, economically and otherwise, throughout the 1960s and 1970s. We had the manufacturing capacity, the gold, and the reserve currency. Baby boomers became adults in this world, and it was an advantage.

Millennials became adults in the 2000s, in a globalized world. We lost our manufacturing jobs overseas, and China quickly became a superpower—and super competitor. However, there are many cultural elements that we have, as millennials, that the baby boomers did not. They did not have Instagram, or Amazon, or even the internet as both a tool and a resource. Each generation has its own set of challenges and bonuses, but, in the end, no one has a choice in the circumstances outside their control—it's what we do with what we have that makes a difference, for ourselves and our children.

Is the risk worth it? Each of us has to decide for ourselves. In doing this, we should consider all of our options, especially if they allow us to lead a more fulfilling life. Currently, everything about the market is pushing us toward independence and sovereignty. The next step is figuring out how to turn what we love doing into a money-making venture.

CHAPTER EIGHT

TURN YOUR HOBBY INTO YOUR BUSINESS

Disneyland is a work of love. We didn't go into Disneyland just with the idea of making money.

—WALT DISNEY

After I fell flat on my face amid the housing market crisis in 2008, Jewel was finally successful in convincing me to follow my passion. I was bringing in a small, steady income from the grocery store, and we were living frugally, but I was depressed. She knew that following financial trends was what I loved doing, and she knew there was potential for me to turn this hobby into a business.

Every Friday, I started airing YouTube videos about investment advice and financial trends for free, with no intention of making money from the venture. It was, at that point, strictly a way for me to find myself again. Purchasing a Logitech webcam for twenty dollars was as technologically sophisticated as I became. Not a single one of my first 241 videos was edited. Most of them ended up being around thirty minutes long. If I messed up, even at the eighteen-minute mark, I hit reset and started over.

Fortunately, my errors grew fewer and farther between, and I became more efficient in my presentation, too. Whereas it took me eighteen minutes to say something in my first video, I said everything clearer and in half the time on my second try. As I improved, I enjoyed the process even more. Each Friday morning, I woke up, reviewed all the economic news from the week, then summarized my opinion on various markets. I typically provided an alternative opinion of the economy in 2008 than that of the Federal Reserve. When they said we would avoid the recession, I predicted it; when they said the stock market was safe, I said it was going to decrease by 50 percent.

Google took over YouTube in 2006, but their involvement was not clear until the middle of 2008. This was when they emailed me about their new partner program in which they paid me for running ads on my YouTube show. I completed the necessary paperwork, and within hours, ads displayed on my videos and I was making money.

My first Google payment was only $150, but it felt great. I was making money from a hobby, and I saw potential for more success. Jewel and I took the money and celebrated at Ruth's Chris Steak House, and the next month, we received a check for $250. By 2009, the checks were $2,500 a month.

In March of 2009, a nonprofit organization contacted me about being their spokesperson, which consisted of a six-second advertisement before my videos. I started out making $500 per video; eventually, they paid me $1,000 per video for this commercial. I moved on to create my own newsletter, ending the agreement with the nonprofit and generating even more revenue from advertising. Before long, I was making $6,500 a month from YouTube alone, doing the same weekly videos I did when I started using YouTube as a hobby.

Like everything else that makes money, ideas that are new and different will make the most money. We see this right now with podcasters making hundreds of thousands of dollars every month because they were the first one to hit the air with their subject. From the first personal finance podcasters to the people interviewing the successful and famous, they had an idea, and they capitalized on it when the medium was in its infancy.

Some of the companies we interact with on a daily basis—like Facebook, Instagram, WhatsApp, and Twitter—did not even exist much more than a decade ago. New technology creates new fields and new job descriptions that completely change how we do things. Being a radio host fifteen years ago required training and an actual employer. Today, with five minutes and an iTunes account, we can have our own show and an eventual income.

WHY WE DO IT

Our hobbies tell us a lot about ourselves. They reveal our passions, and what we enjoy about life. We are lucky when we are able to monetize our hobbies, and the world of technology is just one outlet that enables this opportunity. E-commerce website Etsy connects consumers with independent sellers who specialize in custom orders, vintage items, and unique goods. Shoppers can find anything from obsolete toys and home décor, to personalized stamps and handmade quilts. For creative people searching for a convenient and trusted way to open an online shop, Etsy is the answer.

Almost any hobby can be turned into a business. When my son and I went fishing during a recent trip to Austin, we hired an instructor to show us the appropriate technique. He was slightly older than me, maybe in his forties, and he clearly knew how to fish.

"How many days a week do you fish?" I asked.

"Usually four days a week with clients, and on the weekends by myself," he answered.

That shocked me. It was a lot of fishing time, especially for someone nearing middle age. He had to have a *real* job. I asked him what he did for a living.

He smiled and looked out at the water toward the end of his fishing line. "This *is* what I do. It's all I do for a living. I worked as an executive at Home Depot for years, and then I accepted another executive position at Target. I was in charge of opening new stores all over the world."

He told me that one day he reflected on his life and realized he was spending his best years on an airplane. He was constantly leaving his family for his travels. When he was not traveling, he was still working. Eventually, he decided to take a break, so for six months, he fished every day. Before long, he began advertising fishing lessons on Craigslist as a hobby. Eventually he had a business, and over the course of the six-month-break, he generated as much revenue from his new venture as he did from his executive position at Target. He resigned from Target and never looked back.

I was in total disbelief. I was no stranger to monetizing a hobby, but I didn't realize that someone could make a serious income from an activity like fishing. At first, it didn't make sense, but after some thinking, it made more sense than anything else I'd heard in a long time. Instead of waiting until he was sixty-five and retired, he chose to live his life how he wanted now, despite our society's rules telling him otherwise.

That's the trick to monetizing a hobby, and it's simple: how do we enjoy our lives, and how do we make money from that enjoyment?

I see this strategy work on a different level with my kids. Our son, for instance, loves dinosaurs, so we give him books about dinosaurs. When our daughter loves a song she hears on the radio, we print out the lyrics and she uses them to practice reading. She went from dreading the practice of reading to loving it, simply because she needed to read things she enjoyed.

We have to take these techniques and apply them to ourselves as adults to figure out our interests and passions again. The older we become, the easier it is to forget them. Once we are in touch with who we are again, there are many ways to monetize what we love, whether it's teaching, consulting, or simply setting up a business where people can join you in your favorite hobby.

My family and I participated in Orca Dreams one summer in Vancouver, where we watched orcas and humpbacks every day. The company is owned by a husband and wife team who take whale-watchers on daily tours, either by kayak or on their boat. They love whales, and now they get to spend their summers watching them all day—and making a significant income from it. They take winters off and travel to Africa, something else they prioritize and enjoy.

HOW WE DO IT

Starting a business is not as complicated as many think. Employees do not get the tax benefits of businesses, and, as we've discussed, creating your own business makes more financial sense in the long run.

Culturally, we look at starting a business as a risky venture. We definitely see business ownership as riskier than employment. However, we fail in both scenarios, whether we are fired from our job, or a business that we start is unsuccessful. For some reason, employees never fail in our mass consciousness, but businesses do.

Employees act as their own little business, and they have

essentially committed to their employer. Businesses, on the other hand, are open relationships. As a business, you may have multiple clients and follow opportunities where they take you.

The easiest way to start your own business is by becoming an independent contractor with your current employer, especially if you work for a private entity. By simply approaching them with a plan to become a freelancer, you might be able to negotiate better working conditions and more money for both parties involved. Perhaps you prefer to work from home or go to the office for a limited time each week. We know that some employers, who would be able to eliminate the obligations of healthcare and retirement, might be interested in this prospect.

Also, business owners have a way of connecting with one another on a different level, most likely because we are in the minority. They respect and understand the courage it takes to get off the ground as an independent contractor. They might be willing to review your proposal because they see how they can benefit from it; and, on the other hand, they may not. If they prefer to keep you as an employee, you have a choice to make—to keep working for them, or to quit. With the prospect of being turned down as the only real downside, there's nothing to hold you back from having the talk. Even in this case, your employer might still respect you more for trying to control your destiny. I've been approached by several employees who want to start their own business, and not only do I hire them as contractors, I normally become a financier, as well. It's important for people to take this step, and I want to assist them in any way possible.

STARTING A BUSINESS 101

It's easier than ever to register as a business and be up and running in no time. Depending on your business or career, the following steps may not be mandatory; however, it's important to consider them as you venture into the world of proprietorship.

Start as a sole proprietor by registering as a "doing business as," or a DBA, with your city government. Apply online and pay the registration fee of one hundred dollars to start the process. Filing taxes as a DBA requires your social security number, which serves as your tax identification. You only need to register as a DBA if your business has a storefront.

Starting a business as an LLC is more complicated, but it also provides more protection. This "corporate veil," as it is called, allows you to keep your business separate from yourself, personally. If, for example, your business has a lot of inventory and requires using credit, it's smart to file as an LLC to protect your personal credit score in case something happens to your inventory or credit. Also, if you run a high-risk business, such as a trampoline park for kids, it's a good idea to work with a corporation so that the corporation, in fact, owns the business. If someone sustains an injury there, your corporate insurance will cover the business, but if that insurance were exhausted, having your own LLC would protect you from someone holding you personally liable.

Always keep your personal protection in mind. Start a credit card, bank account, Google AdSense, and Amazon account exclusively for the business. This helps keep you aware of your income and expenses, and it's helpful in the case of an IRS audit.

If you do not like keeping track of paperwork or filing things with the government, try to set yourself up as a sole proprietor or, at most, an LLC. It's simpler and normally covers every small-business need. Corporations have board meetings where fees are collected, even if you are the only board member. Then, local governments must be notified of these meetings, the proceedings, and the fees collected.

In an internet-based business, you might also be able to avoid a sole proprietorship or LLC establishment. Always consult a tax accountant to help you determine that you are maximizing the revenue you generate, and that you're not overpaying in taxes.

Have a plan, a schedule, and a budget to keep you, and the business, on track.

MONETIZING PASSION

Whether your business efforts are on social networking sites or you host your own blog, there are several ways to make money. The easiest way is simply to establish a Google AdSense account that enables you to advertise with Google. They provide a link or banner to display on a Facebook page or website, based on their algorithms and the cookies they collect on your audience. If they know that your audience is interested in purchasing gold, they will display gold ads; if the data they collect shows that someone is interested in hair treatments, they will run a hair treatment advertisement. Google handles everything; you simply collect payment from Google.

If you are interested in proactive advertising and making more money than what is possible with Google AdSense, affiliate marketing is also a good avenue. Simply do an online search for "affiliate marketing" and discover the advertising options that interest you. Some marketers run an advertisement for a product on your website, and if someone purchases that product, you receive a commission check. Others advertise services, such as healthcare, where a provider has a link on your website. If someone becomes their patient or customer, you receive an affiliate fee or bonus. This payment is normally around thirty dollars, so while it's not a lot, it's still an income that requires no effort on your part.

Google AdSense and affiliate marketing are both great ways to monetize a hobby. It's also possible to physically find a client interested in advertising with you. Remember that your efforts will overlap. Cross-marketing between Facebook, Instagram, Twitter, and YouTube, for instance, happens naturally when you are connected on all forums, and it's a good way to unite your audience and solidify your brand. If you ultimately start your own website, blog, or podcast, all cross-marketing should funnel back to the biggest money-maker. If this is your podcast, all efforts should focus on bringing interest and revenue there.

No matter where I advertise, I always direct people back to my website for Future Money Trends—this is my business, and I make my money from advertising. The larger my audience, the more money I make. It's easy to increase your audience numbers by airing more podcasts, or by advertising on social networking sites.

AVOIDING THE PITFALLS

Working for yourself and starting your own business means that you wear many hats. You are the accountant, the salesperson, the janitor, and the manager of everything. It's important to get help where you need it, and to delegate to experts as frequently as possible.

For instance, if you find that producing invoices eats away at your day, it's important to find a bookkeeper. You also don't want to dedicate your time to cleaning, even if it's just an hour a week. The more experts you hire, the better, even if you have to rely on yourself for all these responsibilities in the beginning. The first website I built for FutureMoneyTrends.com was a disaster. It didn't take me long to hire a web page developer and a videographer.

If you have a choice and you have the available resources,

hire others to get the job done right. Every business needs advisors and counsel, whether it's for negotiating taxes or legal advice, or to set up a disclaimer. Don't try to cut corners and save money by thinking you can run a business without input.

Of course, you want to do all of this with your budget in mind. Don't forget that it's a good idea to start your business with a shoestring budget. Your business should be profitable before you pour large sums of money into it. Nothing is worse than spending your entire savings to establish your business, only to see it fail six months after it opens.

OVERDELIVERING

Now that you've started your business, the next step is in figuring out how to be successful when the stability of your business and lifestyle is banking on it.

I consider the first rule of capitalism to be the premise of overdelivering. The success of every business, whether it consists of one employee or one hundred, hinges on the value it delivers. The more value delivered, the more money made.

Not only do we want to overdeliver, we want to overpromise, as well. I learned this from famed American entrepreneur James Altucher, who believes that nothing generates more creativity than challenges. Striving toward exceptionalism in everything we do is vital, but especially if we are serving others.

What made McDonald's renowned was not their amazing food but their concept of fast service. When the restaurant first opened in San Bernardino, California, they made fresh cheeseburgers and excellent milkshakes that everyone loved, but it was their speed that truly impressed patrons. Over the years, their food and its quality have changed, but their promise of fast food has not. In-N-Out Burger, on the other hand, overdelivers in quality; if this changes, they will surely be out of business.

Disney and Costco are also examples of businesses that focus on overdelivering. If you have been to a Disney park, you know that Disney embodies this concept. Disney parks are the epitome of clean and convenient, with FastPass kiosks that always work, food vendors who are easily accessible, and trash cans that are never far from reach, no matter where you are in the park. In fact, Walt Disney took the time to sit on benches at fairs and other theme parks and counted the number of steps visitors took before they gave up and threw their garbage on the ground. This is the kind of elevated consumer thinking that all business owners should emulate.

I feel good about shopping at Costco every time I visit. The stores are always clean, and I feel good knowing that I'm getting the best price available for their products. Also, I can return anything I buy from them at any time, for whatever reason. To me, this demonstrates their commitment to good service and high-quality products.

Any time we start a business, even if it's as a part-time freelancer, we should ask what our customers need from us. Do they need speed, or overdelivery in service? If we are producing a product, do we stand behind that product, through thick and thin? Are we offering any guarantees? Most importantly, we need to ask ourselves how we can overdeliver in a way that makes customers feel positive about interacting with us. How do we make them *want* to interact with us, rather than simply need us? This is how we create success for ourselves in the long run, and how we enjoy our lives, too.

You will notice that when you start focusing on the customer and the quality of service you provide, you will make more money. Concentrating on the money part of the equation is almost a distraction.

Referrals and traffic increased significantly for Future-MoneyTrends.com when I stopped trying to figure out the "correct" equation for a successful, money-making business. At one point, I became obsessed with the placement of our advertisement banners. Was it better in the middle of the website, or in the right corner? How could we maximize our time and effort to make money from this addition? I finally realized that all my concern was a waste of time. I decided to relax with everything related to the business, and the personal finance letter became increasingly personal and relatable. I shared all my financial screw-ups and embarrassing stories, from when I lost $165,000 on a real estate deal, to the moment I stepped into the bankruptcy attorney's office. The more I opened up to readers, the more subscriptions and website traffic we got, and our ad revenue soared. Also, I was happier. It was liberating to share my stories with people, and to see that they actually connected with me and the business better.

FACING THE CHALLENGES

Businesses are ultimately solution providers. Being a business owner should be hard, even if you own and are the sole employee of a one-man shop. There are constant challenges in entrepreneurship, but your investment of time, money, and passion is worth it when you provide the right solutions and reap the financial benefits. You have to believe in your ideas and that you will succeed. Don't be afraid of failure because failure is inevitable. If you distribute a mailer for advertising purposes or if you purchase an ad on a popular website and none of your efforts increase revenue, learn from your first approach and commit to trying something else.

This also helps you in establishing the right mindset for business ownership. You want to respect your business, so that you can ensure that others respect your business, as well. Setting up boundaries is important, especially if you work from home. Before I established my boundaries, people called all day and stopped by unannounced because they knew I worked from home. While you want to spend time with a friend who visits or take a phone call with that family member who is having a hard time, these are business hours in your day that should be dedicated to the success of your business.

Great businesses are made when we never stop trying to deliver more value to our customers. We learn in school that mistakes can be irreversible errors; however, I see mistakes as opportunities to learn. I've failed countless times with my business endeavors. My videos were less than impressive in the beginning, and I've had many real estate deals fall short of closing. I know, however, that it is this kind of failure that makes a business great in the end.

The good news is that when we experience failure, we're in good company. Colonel Harland David Sanders, the founder of Kentucky Fried Chicken, was living in his car when he repeatedly failed to sell his recipe for fried chicken throughout North America. More than one thousand restaurants turned him down, but that didn't stop him. It just took one restaurant to give him a chance, and when they did, the other thousand realized that *they* made a mistake.

Teaching our kids these lessons is just as important as learning them ourselves. By investing differently, ditching retirement, and embracing what we love, we may have figured out the equation for happiness in the twenty-first century. Possibly the most important thing we pass on to future generations, however, is *how* we think about wealth today.

CHAPTER NINE

DO AS I SAY, *AND* AS I DO

Children are sponges—they are going to absorb whatever is around them, so we need to be intentional about what surrounds them.

—DAVE RAMSEY

When my father passed away, I kept his checkbook as a memento—I'd never seen anything like it. It was a detailed ledger of every penny he spent, from ten dollars at Chipotle, to forty dollars for gasoline. He was a master budgeter, and he always made sure his funds were allocated properly.

My father had to start over in life after my parents divorced when I was twelve. I lived with him, and I distinctly remember residing in an empty condo for months.

He made a decent middle-class salary, but my parents did not have much money saved, and the divorce set him back financially. First, we brought in bean bag chairs; then, eventually, a kitchen table, followed by a TV.

He never rushed his purchases. We went to Sears and Montgomery Ward, price checking and making sure he was getting a fair price. We used a coupon booklet everywhere we went, and we always had the competitor's catalog with us to show the salesperson that we could get a better deal across the street.

I learned great budgeting and allocation skills from my dad. He taught me how to be disciplined with money and that life can change abruptly, so we have to be prepared. He routinely quoted King James from the Book of Proverbs 18:21, saying, "Death and life are in the tongue; and they that love it should eat the fruit thereof." I never understood what he meant until I was an adult. My father was fond of telling me to never think negatively, since our thoughts attract and form the energy in our lives. Later, when I read books by Tony Robbins and Napoleon Hill, I realized that there *is* something to be said for thinking positively and absorbing the good.

Finding wealth, stability, and financial balance is directly related to achieving this positive mindset. When you declare good things, good things happen, financially and otherwise.

As a family, my kids, wife, and I acknowledge the positive things in our life out loud. In fact, it's part of my kids' routine when they brush their teeth every morning. They say their name and list all the different things about themselves that make them special. Our oldest daughter, for instance, states her name, followed by the fact that she's a winner, she's smart, and she's unique. I then ask my kids what they love about their favorite superheroes. For our daughter, it's Wonder Woman's strength and beauty. She's able to tie that to her own characteristics and see how she's a superhero, too.

We learn to take these steps in our lives as adults from self-help books. Why not create this mindset when we're young and can benefit from it for the rest of our lives?

WHAT NO ONE TAUGHT US

As millennials, understanding how our mindset impacts every aspect of our lives is something we didn't learn in our youth. In fact, we learned little about savings plans or investment options, and it's clear we didn't learn about necessity versus desire in consumerism. Imagine understanding what investment looks like outside Wall Street as a young adult, or why a budget is important, and how to make it fit your lifestyle. Equipped with this knowledge, would your financial history be different? More importantly, would your entire life be different?

Unfortunately, we still lack these tangible skills in the classroom today. Public schools spend limited hours on financial education, let alone how self-esteem and finances are intertwined. This is a big problem, and it's starting to show in our society. Debt levels are outrageous, and it's normal now for the average citizen to live in the midst of a financial mess. Ultimately, all problems lead back to the decisions we make. The bank may approve us for a 16.9 percent APR credit card, but it's our decision to use that credit card. We cannot place the responsibility for that upon the bank, retailer, or government.

I learned how to write checks in sixth grade. One hour in my high school home ec class was dedicated to a discussion about the importance of college and finding a job that offers a 401(k). In four years of high school and thirteen years of public school education total, I received little more than an hour's worth of instruction about finances. I didn't learn about the history of money, or about the treasury department, monthly budgets, or any of the other financial information that is not only relevant, but *critical* to life in the real world.

School is the perfect environment to learn about finances.

Why didn't our math classes include real-life financial scenarios? Why didn't they add dollar symbols to some of the numbers, and have us interact with one another in mock retail and business transactions? Any small effort from us that gives our kids insight into the financial world will immediately provide them with a competitive edge in life. We learn how to hold a pencil and how to use a computer, but after learning math, reading, writing, and delivering speeches, so much of school curriculum is filler material. There are many fillers in the school system, just as there are many fillers in life.

Regardless of whether or not we choose a career in finance, everyone must understand how money works. Eventually, we grow up, apply for credit cards, and collect student loans. We live in a debt economy and we are lured into financing everything. For example, we score a better deal on a car if we finance it through the dealer's lender. The dealer will even sell it to us for nothing down, as long as we purchase the car on their terms. This is just one of many ways for us to get into financial trouble, even at a young age. Still, for the first twenty years of our lives, no one talks to us about money.

Cambridge University recently released a study showing that people establish their financial habits by age seven. Anyone who has taught a child anything knows that the best way for them to learn is by watching others. According to linguistic professor Jurgen Meisel, a child younger than five can learn two or three languages without much effort. By fifteen, it's difficult to learn even one language. Keep this in mind, as a parent. Our kids are watching us, and they're learning how to function in the world from our behavior.

Prior to the freelance economy, one or both parents typically left the house for work every day. They were not around to discuss finances, and especially not with the kids. Even today, many parents feel that they do not have the proper background to teach their kids about finances.

In our house, we regularly talk about money, and we talk about all of it—the good, the bad, and the ugly. Nothing is held back. This transparency has provided a great lesson for our kids. If we are in the middle of a real estate transaction, Jewel and I talk about the numbers involved. If we win or lose on a stock, we talk about that. It's a normal part of our day, often discussed at the dinner table.

This, of course, is very different from the way most of us were taught, when old rules of decorum told us that we should not discuss money at mealtimes. I think it is healthy and important that we are transparent about our money, especially with our family. In fact, it can be a relief to realize that others have similar challenges, whether they are family or friends. Discussing money with others is actually good, as is sharing our life lessons with our kids, every day.

When our kids know about household bills and the price of the items they use, they begin to connect the dots. This is their introduction to the real world.

THE LESSONS KIDS NEED TO LEARN

We live in a time when it is important that our children learn a sustainable lifestyle, both by decreasing waste and in respecting the resources they have. If our son leaves the lights on in his room, we issue him a ten-cent tax. After all, he is old enough to understand that energy is an expensive, valuable resource that should not be wasted. We want them to know that real wealth includes respecting what we have; and we want them to know that waste is expensive, too.

As parents and grandparents, aunts and uncles, we have a lot to teach our kids. While it's a big responsibility, we can increase our own awareness of how we look at everything that has to do with wealth in our lives. This includes how we use the tool of money, how we plan for the future, and what wealth means to us. My hope is that the previous chapters have provided these moments of reflection for you. Moving forward, I would like to show you what my wife and I teach our kids about money, wealth, and living to our fullest potential.

THE IMPORTANCE OF A BANK ACCOUNT

Our kids have their own bank accounts. It's a nice educational tool that introduces them to the banking system. When they receive a check in the mail for their birthdays, it's exciting for them to go to the bank and deposit their money.

As we have decreased our use of checks as a society, we also are beginning to eliminate the bank from our lives, as well. This may not seem like an entirely negative concept, but it encourages our dependence on credit and overspending. If we go to the store with our child and they want a bike that costs $300, for instance, we have a choice to make. We can either buy the bike or not. If we decide against it, we typically say that we cannot afford it, or it's too expensive. However, it is more constructive to explain to our kids *why* we are not buying the bike that day. Maybe we suggest other uses for the money, like saving for a trip to Walt Disney World or going to a nice dinner at their favorite restaurant. It's good for kids to learn that every dollar spent is taken from somewhere else.

In the book *The Davis Dynasty*, John Rothchild talks about how Chris Davis's family made billions from stock investments. Rothchild shares many Davis family stories, including one when Chris was a child and his frugal grandfather took him out to spend the day together. Chris asked him if he could buy a hot dog during this outing, and his grandfather responded with an explanation of compounding interest. He told him that if they saved the dollar they would spend on the hot dog, that dollar might be worth $25,000 in fifty years. Did he really want a hot dog that costs $25,000? The moral of the story was two-fold: even a dollar amounts to something; and, if you spend the day with Chris's grandfather, bring your own money.

DELAYED GRATIFICATION

Some of the best advice we can give our children—financial or otherwise—is common sense. Learning the simple habit of saving money is a great place to start.

Countless studies show that learning the importance of delayed gratification pays off in the long run. One of the most famous of these studies came from Harvard, where kids were offered one marshmallow immediately, or two if they waited fifteen minutes. Interestingly, after following the kids for two decades, researchers found that those willing to wait scored higher on their SATs, achieved higher salaries, and even experienced better marriages.

Delayed gratification is a skill we must practice and exercise to use it at its fullest potential, much like a muscle in our body. It is a skill best learned when we are young. The best place to practice delayed gratification is at the grocery store, where shelves lined with toys and checkout aisles full of candy entice kids at every turn.

It's easier for kids to save money when it's a gift, but what about the money earned from a lemonade stand, or from babysitting for a neighbor? No matter where their money comes from, kids have to learn the value of saving. Everyone has heard the saying that our money is "burning a hole in our pocket," and there is truth to that. When we have "extra" money, our natural instinct is to spend all of it. However, once we learn to spend now and save later, we build a habit that is almost impossible to break. Kids, in particular, quickly learn that they *deserve* instant gratification, and that they can face the consequences later.

Most of us know what the urge to spend feels like and how hard it is to fight it, especially when we learned the habit of spending at a young age. This is why we need to teach our kids the importance of saving and model good financial behavior, as well. *We* have to be disciplined shoppers, and *we* have to look for the best deals every time we shop or spend money. Kids learn the most from what they see in practice every day, not from what they are taught once or twice a year.

Look at the people involved in your children's lives. It's fun for family and friends to spoil our kids, but this also presents an opportunity for learning. Kids who practice gratitude and appreciate what they have can start to truly understand the concept of wealth and the real value of a dollar.

These lessons are not always convenient for us to teach, as parents. If we go to Target to purchase a toy our child wants only to find that it is sold out, what do we do? Instead of settling on another toy that is conveniently located in the next aisle, we should take them to Walmart or look online, to see if it is available elsewhere. One of the worst lessons we can teach our kids is to settle. This only reinforces the immediate gratification that will surely wear off quickly.

Our kids have no choice but to save half of everything they make, whether it's profit from a lemonade stand, or the money they earn from completing their weekly chores. When they turn seven, I allow them to make stock-purchasing decisions, but when they are younger, they put half their money in a drawer and take the other half to spend, if they choose. If they do not spend it that day, they often forget about it and simply put in their drawer with the rest of their savings. Automatic saving is a great lesson to learn. While their savings will not earn interest money in their sock drawer, it is teaching them the principle of compounding wealth. There is nothing more rewarding than seeing your savings grow. It can almost be addicting.

When they finally save one hundred dollars, I'll swap their change for a crisp hundred-dollar bill, which becomes its own reward. This reinforces the idea that saving a portion of what we earn is important. Our oldest son even purchases silver coins, an idea that I supported because I want him to *feel* the currency in his hands, and to realize that it has actual value. When we realize the value of something, it becomes harder to part with it. If you asked him to use his silver to buy a new skateboard he wants, he would think twice. Although the silver simply sits in his drawer, he understands how precious it is.

THE FUNDAMENTALS OF INVESTMENT

When I started teaching the kids about the stock market, I taught them why particular companies are a better investment than others. Our son is old enough to make decisions about stocks that interest him, so he looks for companies worth his investment. At the ExxonMobil gas station recently, he asked if we could purchase their stock because the business is always clean and convenient. When the kids set up lemonade stands, he takes his money—sometimes $200 or more—and buys additional Disney stock for the shares my wife and I bought for them already. Our kids are starting to understand that it's possible to own pieces of businesses and build wealth with investments, setting them up for the mindset that multiple streams of income are important.

We opened a brokerage account for our son when he turned eight, and we put a portion of his savings in this account. This $300 allows him to buy and sell stocks, with adult supervision. It is typically a better idea to purchase a Vanguard 500 and track it to remain at $500; however, we bought individual stocks and I used our purchases as lessons.

Our son chose to buy stocks from Costco, Disney, Target, and ExxonMobil—all companies he knows. I once told him that I purchased stock in Kimberly-Clark, the toilet paper makers, and he loved the idea. The next time he made money, *he* wanted to purchase Kimberly-Clark, as well. He checks his account weekly to see how his stocks are performing. While he may be going through the motions right now, he is also learning how business and investment work, at a basic level.

I am able to teach our kids beneficial lessons from our investments, not only from the money collection side but also from allowing them to see how I manage my business relationships. When a tenant has a foundation problem, I explain the issue to the kids and tell them why it's a problem. I ask them if we should fix the problem immediately or wait six months. They learn that while our properties are investments, they also are a business and that we consider the tenants our clients.

KIDS AND ENTREPRENEURSHIP

In addition to investments, it is important for kids to learn about the value of entrepreneurship. Many banks host entrepreneur fairs for kids all over the country. While largely unknown, these fairs are growing in popularity, especially amongst the homeschool crowd.

USING BOARD GAMES TO TEACH KIDS ABOUT INVESTMENT

Everyone I know has played the board game Monopoly. Whether you love it or hate it, it is beneficial for kids. Hasbro even makes a version for kids called Monopoly Junior that children as young as three can play. I typically replace Monopoly money with real cash, so that the game is a closer parallel to real life.

Robert Kiyosaki, author of *Rich Dad, Poor Dad*, started writing his book as a game manual for his game, Cashflow. As with Monopoly, Kiyosaki designed a standard game and a game for children, with the object of the game being to make sure their passive income pays for all their expenses. You follow a simple circle, called the Rat Race, where you have the opportunity to buy liabilities like boats and vehicles, in addition to investments like stocks, rental properties, and businesses. Everyone receives a financial statement, and everyone has a career and income.

What makes Cashflow different from other financial games is that it's not fair, just like life. Some players are janitors, while others are doctors and lawyers. The janitor might have an annual income of $30,000, but because of good decisions he can make throughout the game—maybe he has low rent and controls his bills—he can win the game by becoming financially independent quicker than the lawyers and doctors. The goal is also to escape the Rat Race, or the nine-to-five routine, by purchasing the right assets.

I like these games because I think it is important that kids learn accountability. They have to achieve their own success and experience their own failures. The sooner, the better.

Kids are invited to make food to sell, like cookies or lemonade, or make a toy, like the slime that every parent knows too well. They gather in a parking lot, set up their business stand, and sell their product for two hours. It's nice for the kids to make money, but the other benefits outweigh anything they earn. One of the most important things they learn is to overcome any fears they have about selling and pitching to others. Whether we apply for a job or pitch an idea to a client, we must know not only how to sell as adults but how to be comfortable with the process.

The money the kids make at these fairs is an additional benefit. They love playing with money, and the entire process is fun for them. We extend their experience by having our kids use their own money to purchase the materials they need for their business. If they have a lemonade stand, they purchase the sugar, lemons, cups, and napkins. We keep their receipt and compare it to the money they made at the fair. Perhaps they spent twenty-eight dollars at the store and made thirty dollars at the fair. They are profitable! On good days, they can bring in close to eighty dollars.

We try to figure out why they sell more on some days than on others, which allows us to introduce the idea of marketing. They use their creativity to make signs and to figure out ways to attract customers. Sometimes they give away a balloon with every lemonade purchase, or they offer a reduced price for popcorn. This makes the process more interesting for them, and it teaches them valuable skills beyond finance and sales.

It's good for kids to recognize what makes a business great. This will make them better investors when they are older, and they will understand why good business values are important, whether or not they decide to become business owners themselves. Do they want their customers to have the Costco experience, or do they want to operate like every cell phone provider out there, making customers wait hours for a new phone? They should know what being a consumer means and what it feels like, especially when they are young. Not only does it fuel ideas for creative entrepreneurship, but it teaches them about finances and the economy.

When we were in Italy last summer, we bought the kids a toy at a local store that broke within minutes. We returned it to the store, but the manager did not want to take it back or replace it. As we left, I asked the kids a question I ask them all the time when we shop: did that business underdeliver or overdeliver? Even our four-year-old was able to identify that the business did not provide a good customer experience. It's important to show our kids the power and opportunity available in the business world, whether they choose to be an employee, an owner, or an investor one day.

If you feel insecure about your financial knowledge, the good news is that the best thing you can do for your kids and their financial future is simply to talk to them. Talk them through your transactions at Starbucks and Target and explain your receipts. If you are stuck in traffic, talk to them about why rush hour exists, and ask them what they want to do when they are older. What kind of career do they want, and what lifestyle makes the most sense to them? It's good for them to know they have options, and that they don't have to drive two hours to work and spend nine hours at a desk every day, despite what their teachers may tell them.

When kids make a decision to spend their money, talk to them about their decision, and let them conduct the exchange. They should know what it feels like to spend money. This way, they will learn how to count their change and review their receipts. They learn about taxes and about the decreasing value of products over time. They may pay sixty dollars for a toy at Target, but in a year, they will not be able to sell it for fifty cents at a garage sale.

We often fail to analyze our own spending. Talking our kids through our experiences only highlights our own actions. If, for example, we make twenty-five dollars an hour but our lunch costs thirty dollars, what did that meal at Chili's *really* cost us? It's more than just a swipe of the credit card; it's an hour of our lives. Were the salad and margarita worth it? Kids understand these concepts when we share the cost of things, and especially when we compare cost versus income. Maybe they make $300 a year between birthday money and lemonade stands. They may think they can buy a Mercedes with it, but it is our responsibility to show them how far their money really goes.

THE GREATEST LESSON OF ALL: GRATITUDE

Since the time our kids began sitting at the kitchen table for meals, we have taken turns sharing what we are grateful for. We do this for breakfast and dinner. In the morning, we ask what made everyone happy the day before; in the evening, we talk about what we are thankful for that day. Big or small, these are things that make us feel gratitude and appreciation. While gratitude and appreciation are powerful states of mind, they are sometimes the most difficult for us to learn.

Being grateful is a healthy mindset. It's hard to be stressed, worried, or angry when we are thinking about what makes us happy and appreciative. This applies to the financial world, as well. We spend smarter, save better, and enjoy our financial prosperity more when we are able to think clearly about our lives and when we take the time to graciously reflect on what we have.

As Americans, we are blessed with cultural prosperity, something our children should understand. When my son once told me that he was having a bad day because he was losing at a game, I responded that if this is his idea of a bad day, he has a pretty good life. I want our kids to know that we cannot take our lifestyle for granted and that there are reasons we want to preserve and respect what we have.

When I see people indulging in excess debt, or buying items they cannot afford, I think that they are wasting their position in this world. I frequently find myself reminding our kids that our life is great and that even if we were poor, our life would still be much better than what others experience all over the world. Keeping kids grounded is important, both as a general life lesson and as a way for them to appreciate the power of their financial state. A big part of saving money is not wasting it in the first place. If we can incorporate gratitude into their daily lives and help them understand the depth of wealth as a concept, they are less likely to make bad decisions in the long run because they know what truly matters.

I want our kids to think about what makes them happy every day. When I ask them this question, they usually talk about people in their lives or experiences they remember. Whether it is their family, friends, church, business, or country, people truly make the difference.

Our six-year-old daughter can tell us that the people working at Disneyland set Disney apart from other theme parks, simply because she knows they make her feel happy when she's there. It's often hard to identify, but the quality of almost every experience we have is based on the people involved in it.

Think about the last time you tipped a server an amazing tip, versus the time you left the restaurant and tipped nothing, angry that there was even a tip line included. Our attitude is everything; if we can learn the importance of a positive attitude and outlook when we are young, we are more likely to experience success later. After all, *we* are the biggest income producer in our lives, not our investments, or the people who support us. It's our attitude toward everything, and everyone, that makes the difference.

CONCLUSION

Ten years ago, my net worth was about $20,000. I worked a dead-end job, and I saw my wife two hours every day. Today, I'm financially free. I've taken my kids to ten countries, and I see my wife for the majority of every day. I changed not only how I look at finances, but how I want to spend my life.

You can do this. I know because I did it, despite the odds. I don't have a degree or a special network. My family name is not Rockefeller or Hearst. However, we live in an era of opportunity, in a country that promotes freedom. We have access to crowdfunding, whole life insurance policies, cryptocurrency, and precious metals. There are countless ways for us to invest, and it's easier than ever to learn about them.

We are mobile, as a culture. We can work remotely and

invest remotely. If we want to buy real estate in a foreign country, we can do that without visiting the location. Technology has opened doors and enabled us to thrive. Corporations are born in a day, and people who never imagined themselves as entrepreneurs are starting their own businesses.

The conventional plan of our past is outdated. It's time we accept that and move on. For years, the millionaires and billionaires of our society have focused on owning multiple streams of income. This was their path to financial freedom, and it's ours.

Most of us are understandably afraid of risks. However, our risk assessment is faulty. Employment benefits are no longer guaranteed, and we cannot rely on our 401(k) and Social Security to carry us to retirement. It's time to find our independence, in our investments and in our careers. Fortunately, our best investment options are off Wall Street and we need look no further than ourselves to find the work that makes us happy.

What does *your* future hold?

As I sat in the office of the bankruptcy attorney with my wife, I knew my future was better than it seemed in that moment. I had to make changes. I had to eliminate wasteful spending, forget peer pressure, and make my own path. It wasn't easy, but I'm proud of the life we have built. Most importantly, I'm not worried about the future.

Becoming financially independent means buying our freedom. I bought mine—now it's your turn.

ACKNOWLEDGEMENTS

First and foremost, I want to thank my wife. Since we first met at sixteen, her encouragement, love, and patience have brought us to where we are today.

With this book, I want to honor my late father, who showed me how to be a good dad. His commitment to fatherhood and love for his family are his legacy, treasures he left behind for every generation after him.

A big thank you goes out to my children, who are now regularly beating me in daily games of Monopoly, Cashflow, and Net Worth; and to my sisters, who have always been overwhelmingly supportive of me, even in the worst of times.

My mother has sent me prayers and positive energy every single day of my life, and I'm eternally grateful to her.

I would also like to thank the following people who have supported me, influenced me, and motivated me to be my best:

Lior Gantz and Kenneth Ameduri, my male soulmates and business partners.

My assistant, Tasha, whose passion and dedication helped me make this book possible.

J & H, whose love and support throughout these last two decades has meant the world to me.

The Lindsey family—the warmth of their entire family is beautiful.

My "rich dad," Mr. Petermann, whose guidance and unconventional approach has always inspired me.

Our Texas family: Gordon, Kris, Randy, Justin, and Alton.

Keith Neumeyer, a great mentor and friend who has truly changed my life for the better.

Amir Adnani, who taught me how to negotiate and demand excellence.

Finally, I'm grateful for all the obstacles and challenges

in my life. Sometimes the most difficult experiences lead to the greatest blessings.

ABOUT THE AUTHOR

DANIEL AMEDURI is a self-made multi-millionaire, a full-time skeptic of conventional thought, and a proud father of three. He is the co-founder of FutureMoney-Trends.com, which, with nearly 150,000 subscribers, is the most widely recognized online authority in investment ideas and economic advice. He's been featured in *The Wall Street Journal*, on *ABC World News Tonight*, and on Russia Today TV. Daniel correctly predicted the collapse of Lehman Brothers, AIG, and Washington Mutual on "Vision Victory," the YouTube channel he launched in 2007 and which now has had more than thirteen million views.

Made in the USA
Monee, IL
11 September 2019